How To Gamble

At The Casinos

Without

Getting Plucked

Like A Chicken

by

James Harrison Ford

Published by
El Paso Norte Press
El Paso, Texas

How To Gamble At The Casinos
Without Getting Plucked Like A Chicken

by James Harrison Ford

First Edition – August 2004

Published by
EL Paso Norte Press
404 Christopher Ave
El Paso, Texas 79912

ISBN 0-9760726-0-2
Library of Congress Control Number: 2004096286
Printed in the United States of America

Preface

To keep from getting plucked like a chicken at the casinos, you should avoid acting like you just fell off the turnip truck. You need to appreciate, and take advantage of, the vast storehouse of information that has been accumulated about gambling. The universe didn't begin when you opened your eyes this morning. Unless you are truly a genius, there is nothing you have ever considered that some sharp cookie out there hasn't already worked out to six decimal places. Basically, you need to educate yourself: Hit the books, like this one.

However, even if you become a fountain of gambling knowledge, develop super human computational skills, make sure you find the games with the best percentages, obtain a sufficient bankroll, size your bets a shade below the Optimum Bet Size and play like a virtuoso, when you gamble, you will still lose some of the time. The trick is to win more often than you lose and to enjoy the process.

It is not really necessary to work all that hard at gambling to be relatively successful at it. The application of a little knowledge goes a long way. Avoiding the pitfalls by applying the knowledge that has been built up over the centuries can work wonders. The object of this book is to give you just enough information to make you dangerous; not to yourself, but to the casinos.

If this book helps steer you toward a more profitable and enjoyable gambling experience, then I will consider it a great success. No doubt, as you read through these pages, you will happen upon an occasional statement that you disagree with. Don't let it bother you. No one is perfect. Don't be too hard on yourself.

My confidence is not misplaced. Nothing in this book is new. It is a compilation of remembered lessons and theory tempered by years of experience. If it were of any real consequence, like Newton, I could say: "I have stood on the shoulders of giants." I just wish my memory were good enough for me to credit the correct sources.

The people like Girolamo Cardano (1501 - 1576), Pierre de Fermat (1601 - 1665), Blaise Pascal (1623 - 1662), Christiaan Huygens (1629 - 1695), Jakob Bernoulli (1654 - 1705), Abraham de Moivre (1667 - 1754), Pierre-Simon Laplace (1749 - 1827)... John von Neumann, Roger Baldwin, Herbert Maisel, Wilber Cantey, James McDermott, Allan Wilson, Edward Thorp, Julian Braun, Robert Epstein, Martin Gardner, Peter Griffin, Lenny Frome, Stanford Wong and a host of others, too many to mention, have done all the hard work. Learning and re-learning, sorting out the most applicable information usually requires more than a single lifetime.

This small effort is not intended as any sort of tribute to those whose work has made it possible, but their work is reflected here, in these pages of what attempts to be practical advice. Albert Einstein has been quoted as saying: "The secret to creativity is knowing how to hide your sources." It is for you, the reader, to determine how successful this effort has been.

J. H. Ford
Las Vegas
August 2004

How To Gamble At The Casinos
Without Getting Plucked Like A Chicken

Contents

Contents

Chapter 1 – The Bottom Line

Question: Why do people gamble?
1. For enjoyment
2. For profit
3. Both of the above

There are many more possible answers to the question: "Why do people gamble?" All of them probably apply, at one time or another, to someone or another. However, answer number 1 could probably be stretched to cover most of those other possible answers. The fact is that people are inclined to do a lot of strange things for enjoyment. Take skydiving, bungee jumping, mountain climbing... as examples. Then there are the really bizarre hobbies: square dancing, playing bagpipes and golf. People get enjoyment out of the darnedest things. Sadists enjoy being cruel. Masochists enjoy being punished. Some people even get turned on by making money. As they say: "Different strokes for different folks."

If, for yourself, you answered: "For enjoyment" to the question, then this book will, at best, be a waste of time for you and, at worst, just might diminish your enjoyment. You might read things that you really don't want to know, like: "It's really not bright to jump out of a perfectly good airplane." If your intent is simple enjoyment, then there is nothing this book can teach you. You and only you know what turns you on.

If you answered: "For profit" to the question, then also, this book probably will be of no benefit to you. You undoubtedly already know the best games to play, how to play them correctly and the best places to play them. You will have already read everything about casino gambling you can get your hands on and are checking out this book just to make sure you haven't missed anything. Either you own a casino, are negotiating to build or buy one, or you are some sort of expert. This book is not going to make an expert more of an expert. If you own a casino, you can afford to hire all the experts you need.

If you answered: "Both of the above" to the question, then we have something to work with, assuming you are reading this book to help you become more successful. Gambling can be both enjoyable and profitable, if you do it right.

First, it helps if you know why you are doing what you are doing – going to the casinos and gambling in this case. Examining your expectations and motivations may help you to understand and possibly modify some tendencies that might be keeping you from being a winner.

Several years ago when I was still working for a living, a friend of mine, George, and I decided we needed a small vacation. We took Friday off and got to Atlantic City about midday. Immediately we got onto the tables and luck was with us. Within a few hours both of us had large stacks of chips in front of us. It dawned on me that it might be a good time to quit, so I turned to George and said: "I think it is about time for me to find something to eat." George nodded and said: "Good idea. I'll join you." We cashed out and found a café. Over dinner I asked George; "Do you think we ought to go home early; quit while we're ahead?" George grinned broadly and said: "Naw, let's give it all back." We stayed the whole weekend, had a wonderful time and gave it all back.

That surely wasn't the brightest thing I've ever done, as far as the money was concerned, but we were there to enjoy ourselves, and we did. Few things are more enjoyable to me than gambling on house money. The only thing that could have made it much better would have been for us to have gone home as big winners. We didn't. But we stood a good chance. The best you should ever expect is to stand a good chance.

How many people do you know, or have you ever known, who stand a good chance to make a cash profit from their hobby? No one I have ever known has made any money by skydiving, bungee jumping, mountain climbing, square dancing, or golfing (I have very studiously avoided knowing anyone who plays the bagpipes.)

Gambling tends to get a bad rap because it can cost money, a lot of money, especially if you aren't good at it. In that regard, it is not much different than other types of hobby activities. Take golf for example. Golf can be a very expensive hobby by the time you add it all up: equipment costs, country club dues and/or green fees, special clothing, lawyer fees, court costs and fines. Hobbies can be really expensive and rarely ever turn a profit.

As hobbies go, casino gambling has another feature, in addition to the profit potential, that sets it apart from other hobby activities: comps. The casinos actually give the players free stuff just for playing. The free stuff ranges from free drinks, free meals, free hotel rooms, free merchandise, free limousine service... to just about anything you can think of.

Try to imagine a similar deal with other hobby activities. It is a little like a golf resort having a promotion that offers free golf if you shoot par golf and then, regardless of your score, just for playing at their course they will give you a free lunch. If you play two rounds, they will throw in dinner, a movie and a free night's lodging.

Suppose the deal is: your score determines the amount you get paid or have to pay for your green fee. For every stroke your game is under par, they will give you money. If you play scratch golf, you play for free. However, for every stroke your game is over par you have to pay them and the higher your score, the higher your green fee. I've never heard of a deal like that, but if there was and if I were a good golfer, you know where I'd play.

To carry the analogy out: the games in the chapter titled The Good Games are the breakfast of champions; the games in the chapter titled The Bad Games are like the golfer with a low handicap who sometimes breaks par but mostly shoots a little over; the games in the chapter titled The Ugly Games are strictly duffer stuff.

At the casino, the games you choose to play and how well you play them will determine whether you have a profitable hobby or not. All it takes is a bankroll, a little knowledge and the determination not to be taken advantage of. If you have some money you can afford to gamble with and the ability to use your head for anything other than a hat rack, you have the qualifications to be a successful gambler.

Unlike golf or other physical sporting activities, it doesn't take good hand to eye coordination to gamble well. It hardly takes any physical skill at all. In most casinos, you just have to be able to sit up. Wheelchairs and oxygen bottles are OK. I've never seen anyone play from a stretcher. I have actually seen a blind guy play Blackjack. He was pretty good at it too.

Gambling is one of the few hobbies, short of armed robbery, in which you can come home with more money than you started out with. Of course, luck has a lot to do with it. Absolute amateurs, idiots, drunks and even occasionally an expert can have a good session and come out ahead. Think about it: you get to enjoy yourself, the casinos will give you free stuff and you can make money at it, all at the same time. What a deal!

Or, should we say: What an ideal. It's not always easy...

First and foremost, you must throw away some of your prejudices. "What, me, prejudiced?" you ask, incredulous. Yeah, you. And me, but then that's a different story. You can take it to the bank that there are some things that you believe, that you know to be absolutely true, that are not only wrong, but will keep you from being a successful gambler. Giving them up can be an arduous journey.

My most important credentials for writing this book are the mistakes I have made over the years. Gradually, I have learned how to avoid a lot of the mistakes. I have had to learn most of the lessons the hard way. But, you don't have to. Repent! And save a few of your hard-earned bucks. If you are willing to learn, it's actually pretty easy.

You don't have to be smart enough, or industrious enough, to do a lot of complicated math. You just have to be smart enough to listen to the folks who are. Most of them are nice people. They tend to enjoy fooling around with numbers so much that, if you show a little interest, they will usually share their knowledge with you.

I wish I had been smart enough to check with them earlier in my life. Mostly what this book is about is sharing those borrowed smarts. The lessons were learned, little by little, over a long period of time. At one time or another I have done about every dumb thing you can think of: fallen for every come-on, made every sucker bet, lost the rent money... the list goes on and on.

But, I have gotten better. From years of exposure and experience, I have learned to adjust my unreasonable expectations to the practical realities of casino gambling. It is not easy to trim exorbitant flights of fancy down to the realm of the possible, but that's really where you have to start.

First, you need to find out what the situation really is, not in your dreams, but in real life. Then, you have to be able to cope with what is really possible and what isn't. Most folks don't have a clue.

Walk into any casino and look around at the people playing the slot machines. Take the time to examine the folks at the corner convenience store who are standing in line to buy lottery tickets. What do you see? For the most part you see people who, somewhere in the bottom of their hearts, really believe that they are going to strike it rich. We both know that virtually none of them will.

That doesn't mean that gambling, casino gambling in particular, has nothing to offer. On the contrary, it is quite possible to profit from casino gambling, apart from owning the casino. The probability of getting rich doing it is so unlikely as to be laughable. Also, the probability of making a decent living doing it is pretty small. However, the expectation of enjoying yourself in a pleasant, attractive setting and occasionally coming home with more money than you left with is not unreasonable.

Having reasonable expectations; knowing that there isn't a magic incantation, secret spell, silver bullet or proprietary winning system that will open the Horn of Plenty; is a pretty good place to start. But, that's only the beginning.

You also need to look at the downside; stare into the abyss; come to grips with the worst that can happen and ask yourself if you can afford it. You flat-out have to have an appreciation that sometimes you will lose. There's a saying: "There ain't a hoss that can't be rode, or a cowboy that can't be throwed."

Deal with it. They don't call it gambling for nothing. If you can't afford to lose, don't gamble. Set aside what you can afford to spend on your hobby and expect to spend it. Play the best games, play them well, give yourself a chance to win, enjoy yourself and you will be a real winner whether you make any money at it or not. You need to be careful about harboring expectations that might not be met.

In order to become a successful gambler you have to be willing to accept losses as part of the game. No one can win all the time. Thinking that you should win all the time will only lead to disappointment and possibly promote self-destructive behavior. A reasonable approach to gambling requires some appreciation of the ebb and flow of fortune.

The bottom line is: you need to enjoy doing what it takes to really profit from the experience. There is a Zen-like quality involved in getting down to the details of what it takes to do a thing, like gambling, well. From time to time, you need to hear the music of the game.

The force has to be with you. The force of self-will, that is, or more precisely: self-won't, to not make dumb plays.

Turn it into a game. Find a way to make it fun. Perhaps you can think of yourself as a Jedi warrior, like Luke Skywalker, with whom the force is strong. Maybe you can see yourself as the Jedi master, Obi-Wan Kanobi, or if you are feeling a little weird, Yoda. Careful with the voice though you must be.

If you do it right, you will actually stand a good chance and, from time to time, you will make money at it. If you are very good at it, you can win a little more than half the time and your wins will total up to more than your losses. But, you will still have losing sessions some of the time. When you do, don't panic. Learn to trust the percentages.

Self-discipline is essential to success. This book, and many others, can give you the information about the best games and how to play them, but it is up to you to turn that information into action. If you don't enjoy the challenge of never ever giving in to the temptation of letting the casinos have the percentage on their side, at least until you are playing on their money, then you shouldn't gamble – ever.

If you acquire the essential knowledge and apply it without fail, winning consistently is actually pretty straightforward: Play only when you have the percentage on your side, and then, turn your bankroll into a multitude of small wagers and let the percentage grind the opposition down. When you do it right, it's really not gambling.

Chapter 2 – The Percentage

If you don't know that the percentage is the single most important factor in winning, then you don't know squat. Perhaps Mario Puzo said it best:

> **Percentages never lie. We built all these hotels on percentages. We stay rich on the percentage ... You can lose faith in everything, religion and God, women and love, good and evil, war and peace, you name it. But the percentage will always stand fast.**
>
> (Mario Puzo, *Fools Die*, G.P. Putnam's Sons, New York, 1978, p196, p508)

When the house has an edge of 5%, which is the same thing as 95% payback, it simply means that over many repeated wagers, the house will, on the average, keep five cents out of every dollar wagered. Consider the case of flipping a fair coin. Half the time you win. Half the time you lose. But if I were to have a 5% edge, then whenever you lost you would pay me a dollar, and whenever you won, I would pay you ninety cents. Not a bad deal... for me.

Gambler's Ruin

The effect of the Percentage, in grinding away a bankroll, is known as Gambler's Ruin. Over the long term, after many plays, whoever has the Percentage will ultimately win. The larger the Percentage, the sooner it happens. A big house Percentage will grind you down a lot quicker than a small one. It is an absolute mathematical certainty.

Although in the short term anything that can happen might happen, you can be absolutely certain that in the long-term

Gambler's Ruin will prevail. No one can beat the odds forever.

Take a look at Figures 2-1 and 2-2. They illustrate the point that in the short run anything can happen (Figure 2-1) and over the longer haul, the percentages tend to kick in (Figure 2-2). These graphs show 3 series of random trials where the house has no edge (0%), a 2% edge and a 5.26% advantage. The data shown on Figure 2-1 are just the first set of 200 trials from the larger set of 10,000 trials shown on Figure 2-2.

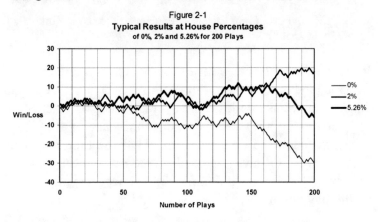

Figure 2-1
Typical Results at House Percentages
of 0%, 2% and 5.26% for 200 Plays

The thin line on Figure 2-1 shows that the player with the best game, the 0% House Edge, is getting the worst of it with a net loss of 30 units after 200 plays. The player with the worst game, against a 5.26% House Edge, the darkest graph line, is only down about 6 units and the player who is working against the 2% disadvantage is actually winning about 18 units after 200 plays; a fairly typical set of results for the short term. Anyone could be ahead or behind after a short set of random trials.

However, as you can see on Figure 2-2, the chickens have pretty much come home to roost by 10,000 plays, although

10,000 plays really isn't long term. The player with the 0% game is about 100 units ahead, the player with the 2% disadvantage is down about 200 units and the player with the 5.26% disadvantage is down a little more than 500 units. As the number of plays continues to increase, the lines will appear to stop wandering and settle in even more closely on values reflecting the various percentages.

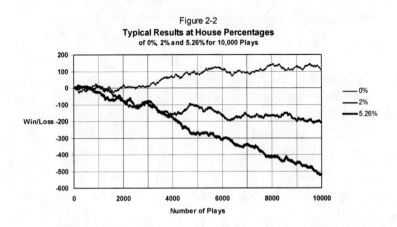

Figure 2-2
Typical Results at House Percentages
of 0%, 2% and 5.26% for 10,000 Plays

The kind of data shown on these figures are fairly typical of "random walk" processes when you take into account a variable amount of bias. How far a drunk, with one pocket stuffed full of quarters, wanders from the straight and narrow depends on the weight of quarters in that pocket.

Gambler's Ruin is a classical bit of mathematics. Although the calculations are relatively simple, the results are quite profound. In addition to showing that whoever has the percentage on his side will ultimately win, Gambler's Ruin calculations also show that the biggest wins, that is, whoever has the biggest bankroll will ultimately grind the other guy down. It's not magic, it's just arithmetic.

The Gambler's Ruin equations are shown here for the sake of completeness and smugness. Now, whenever anyone mentions Gambler's Ruin you can always say: "Yeah, I've got those equations in a book at home somewhere." But, you can relax. You don't need to do anything with them. I'll show you enough worked out examples to make you an expert and then make your eyes glaze over.

The formulas for the probability of being ruined (R) are:

$$\text{For an uneven game:} \quad R = \frac{(q/p)^b - (q/p)^{b+t}}{1 - (q/p)^{b+t}}$$

$$\text{For an even game:} \quad R = 1 - \frac{b}{b + t}$$

where:
> b is the player bankroll,
> p is the probability the player will win,
> q is the probability that the house will win,
> t is the win target (or the minimum house bankroll).

The expected duration (D) of Gambler's Ruin is given by:

$$\text{For an uneven game:} \quad D = \frac{1}{1 - 2p} \left[b - \frac{a(1 - s^b)}{1 - s^a} \right]$$

$$\text{For an even game:} \quad D = b\,t$$

where:
> a is the total stake, b + t; and s = q / p.

Let's be clear here about what we mean by the House Edge or the House Percentage relative to the probability that the house will win. If the house has an edge or Percentage of 2%, it means that they will win 51 times out of 100; so the probability that the house will win is 0.51 and the probability the player will win is 0.49, a difference of 0.02, or 2%.

Take the case where you have $20 and decide to bet $1 at a time until you lose your $20 or double it up before you walk away. What the Gambler's Ruin calculations show, on Table 2-1, is that, if it is an even game, it is just as you would expect: you have a 50-50 chance of winning or losing and, on the average, the final outcome will take about 400 plays before you walk away without your $20 or with a total of $40.

Table 2-1				
Gambler's Ruin				
Assuming a bankroll of 20 units, doubling up against 0%, 3% and 8% House Edge				
Player's Bankroll	Win Target	House Percentage	Probability of Ruin	Average Number of Plays
20	20	0%	50%	400
20	20	3%	79.6%	358
20	20	8%	96.1%	231

For the same $20, again one dollar at a time, if the house has a 3 percent edge, you stand a 76.9% chance of losing your $20 and only a 23.1% chance of winning. It will all be over in about 358 plays.

You think that's bad? Try it when the house has an 8 percent Edge. You stand a 96.1% chance of ruin, with a corresponding 3.9% chance of doubling up. On the average, the resolution to this debacle will take 231 plays.

An 8% house Edge is probably about normal for most slot machines. It is difficult to walk past a row of busy slot machines in almost any casino without hearing someone say: "I wouldn't mind losing so often if I only got a little more play for my money." I have always been tempted to stop and say; "Hey, smarten up. Play something with a smaller House Percentage."

The preceding three examples are relevant only to doubling up your initial stake of 20 units. Don't scoff. Doubling your stake is a real good day's work. If you could do that on the stock market, on even a semi-regular basis, you would soon become a major guru, a legend in your own time. People like Warren Buffet would offer to take you to dinner and try to curry your favor. But that applies only to such endeavors as the stock market. In the world of gambling, almost no one is happy with a paltry doubling of their stake. Time and time again, gamblers get greedy.

It is not at all unusual for someone to start with a relatively small stake and not be willing to walk away as a winner until they have increased their stake at least 10 fold. In the case of a fair wager, where neither side has an edge, the probability of going broke when you try to win $100 with an initial stake of $10 is 90.909%, as shown on Table 2-2.

Table 2-2				
Gambler's Ruin				
Assuming a bankroll of 10 units, to win 100 against 0%, 3% and 5.26% House Edge				
Player's Bankroll	Win Target	House Percentage	Probability of Ruin	Average Number of Plays
10	100	0%	90.909%	1000
10	100	3%	99.888%	329
10	100	5.26%	99.9983%	190

Basically, you will get busted more than 9 times out of 10 when you try it, even when the other guy doesn't have an edge. Note the point: Greed Kills.

It is worse, much worse, when the other side has the Percentage, as in roulette. Consider what the Gambler's Ruin calculations show for a $10 stake, wagered $1 at a time, with a house percentage of 5.26%, when the players have decided to walk away only when they have made $100 or have gone bust: There is a 99.9983% chance of going bust. That means that you will get wiped out 9,999 out of every 10,000 times.

An advertising slogan for one of the games that offers a jackpot payoff of several million dollars for a small wager goes something like: "One pull can change your life." That is very alluring. Like Lee Trevino says: "Well, somebody's got to win these things." The fantasy of hitting The Big One flows through every gambler's dreams.

But, given the large House Percentage, in the back of my mind, I can almost hear the owners, stockholders and the executives who have stock options and profit-sharing plans cheerfully humming: "We're in the money…"

If you go after it with smaller expectations, your odds are much better. When you are willing to risk more, to win less, rather than the other way around, you actually stand a better chance of winning as shown on Table 2-3.

Suppose you start with $20 and again bet it $1 at a time, against a house edge of 3 percent; but this time you would walk away after winning only $10, rather than $20. Now, rather than there being a 79.6% chance of going bust, your chance of busting is 54.1%. That is, rather than having only a 23.1% chance of winning, your odds go up to 45.9%. Sure, it is a smaller reward for a higher amount put at risk, but the odds are much better; not good, but better.

Table 2-3				
Gambler's Ruin				
Assuming a bankroll of 20 units, 3% House Edge, to win 20, 10 or 2 units				
Player's Bankroll	Win Target	House Percentage	Probability of Ruin	Average Number of Plays
20	20	3%	79.6%	358
20	10	3%	54.1%	207
20	2	3%	15.4%	47

Taking that same idea further: consider risking $20, one dollar at a time, to win $2, against a house edge of 3 percent. The gambler's ruin calculation shows an 84.6% probability of winning the $2 with a corresponding risk of losing the $20 being only 15.4%.

Winning $2 is pretty paltry, huh? Well, it is a 10% return on investment. How well are your stocks, bonds and (snort) interest bearing bank accounts doing? Consider then, risking $200 to win $20; then bet $10 a whack, at the same odds. How about risking $2,000 to win $200, betting $100 a pop. Maybe $20,000 to win $2,000... Come on; I thought you wanted to gamble. Remember, you have to give action to get action.

Being happy with a relatively small return is another aspect of the Principle of Biggest Wins. A bigger bankroll, relative to the amount you want to win, can turn a small house percentage into short-term odds that are favorable to the player. The penalty, however, is that the risk-reward ratio is unbalanced. You have to risk a big loss to have a good chance to make a small profit. The simple reality is that it is easier to make a small profit than a large one.

For the mathematicians out there, one of the best measures of the potential profitability of any wager or series of wagers is, of course, the Expected Value. For those who aren't mathematicians, the Expected Value (EV) is the sum of the products of each of the possible outcomes times the corresponding probability of each of the possible outcomes.

For the above cases, when the house has a 3% edge:
When you risk $20 to win $20,
the EV is ($10*0.231- $20*0.769) = -10.76
When you risk $20 to win $10,
the EV is ($5*0.459 - $20*0.541) = -6.23
When you risk $20 to win $ 2,
the EV is ($1*0.846 - $20*0.154) = -1.39

These numbers show that being happy with a smaller return has a better (or less bad) Expected Value, but notice that the house edge of 3 percent still gives the player a long-term negative expectation.

Mathematicians tend to make a big deal out of the effect of how you break up your bankroll, and rightly so. That's one of the reasons mathematicians and gamblers tend to talk about wagers in terms of "units". The effect of breaking your bankroll into various size units is shown on Table 2-4.

Suppose you take that same $20 and intentions to turn it into $40 against that small house edge of only 3% that we talked about earlier. Now rather than betting it $1 at a time, you bet it 50¢ at a time. You have 40 units and are trying to win another 40 units. Running it through the Gambler's Ruin formula, rather than a ruin probability of 76.9% you now have a 91.7% chance of losing, and have turned the merely disastrous into the truly catastrophic.

Want to try for the apocalyptic? Break the $20 down into
quarters. Trying to win 80 units with 80 units against that
tiny house edge of merely 3%, turns the odds of losing your
stake into 99.2%.

Table 2-4				
Gambler's Ruin				
Assuming different bankrolls to double up against a 3% House Edge				
Player's Bankroll	Win Target	House Percentage	Probability of Ruin	Average Number of Plays
20	20	3%	79.6%	358
40	40	3%	91.7%	1112
80	80	3%	99.2%	2623
400	400	3%	99.9999+%	13,333

But wait, it gets worse. You can go for the absolutely,
monumentally, catastrophic, apocalyptic … I'm running
out of descriptive terms here. Try nickels. Trying to double up $20 worth of nickels against a house edge of 3%,
results in a 99.99999996% chance of being busted. It is no
wonder that the casinos love low rollers.

Carrying this "unit effect" to the other extreme, you get the
counterintuitive result that betting the $20 all at one time
will give you the best expectation against that 3% house
edge. In this case, the probability of ruin is only 51.5%,
nearly an even wager.

Given an unfair game (one in which the house has the edge,
not one where they cheat), how can a player maximize his
probability of coming out ahead? Simple… don't play.
Short of not playing, the best a player can do is to be willing
to lose a lot in order to win a little – which still carries a long-
term negative expectation. Or, carried to its logical extreme,
when the player must play a game in which the house has the
mathematical edge, the best strategy is for him/her to collect

everything he/she ever intends to wager and make one big bet, then walk away forever. Only then, against an unfair game, are the odds as close to even as they will ever get.

If you try to tell this to nickel slot players, they will look at you as though you had two or more heads. If, on the other hand, you set about capturing mathematicians, plunking them down at a $1 Roulette table, telling them that they can bet whatever size units they want and if they don't double up $20 they will be mutilated to death. Most likely, 999 out of 1,000 will bet the $20 in one chunk. Of course, they will probably sweat a little, but you can be pretty sure that most of the survivors won't have fooled around with a bunch of piddling little bets.

Without a doubt, the ideal situation is to have both the percentage in your favor and have the biggest bankroll. It takes a lot of really bad luck to lose under those circumstances. With enough money, the mathematics say it is virtually impossible (the rich get richer). It sounds a lot like being the House. But then, not everyone can afford to buy or build a casino. The best most of us can do is to minimize the house edge or squeak out a fractional percentage edge in our favor.

The Gamblers' Ruin calculations show that not only do you need to have the percentage on your side, to have the best chance of winning, you need to have a bigger bankroll than most people would expect. The numbers, and common sense, will tell you that someone with a bankroll that is much bigger than yours has a good chance to take yours away from you if you don't pay attention to the details.

When the chips are really down, it is hard not to agree with the mathematicians. The casinos do. Understanding and using the probabilities will give you the best chance of winning over the long haul. It won't keep you from losing, but it will give you the best chance of winning. There's that word again: chance.

Luck Versus Skill

We are beginning to sneak up on the subject of luck. The percentage, the probability and the odds tell us nothing about that wild card: Luck. It is a short-term phenomenon. Luck can be considered a manifestation of the principle that sooner or later anything that can happen will happen. When your long shot comes in, you are lucky. When your dead-cert loses, you are unlucky. With gambling, skill consists of arranging to have the percentage on your side. There is very little you can do about luck, short of quitting forever when you are ahead, unless you have the percentage on your side.

Gamblers recognize that luck is hard to beat. After taking a "bad beat"; that is losing a bet even though the odds had been on their side, many a gambler has been heard to say: "I'd rather be lucky." Sometimes it takes a lot of plays for the percentages to kick in, but you can be certain they will, given enough plays. My own computer tells me it takes about a quarter of a million blackjack hands for the percentages to begin to solidify.

After a long tiring session to grind out a small win, a professional gambler friend was heard to say: "It took me twenty years to learn the difference between luck and skill. I would rather be lucky." When I pressed him on that point, he grudgingly admitted that having the percentage is more reliable. That's what the casinos try to do.

Personally, one of the reasons I like casinos, particularly Las Vegas casinos, is that some of them offer a few games in which the player, if skillful, can actually have an edge. Yes, I know that sounds strange, but it is true. Don't just take my word for it. Check it out.

The open literature on mathematics, not to mention books on gambling, will verify this point: Some varieties of Blackjack can be beaten. The literature on Blackjack is enormous. Most of it is over-optimistic. Some of it is wrong. Further along, I shall endeavor to give you the straight poop.

Not all casinos offer games in which the player can gain the percentage by skillful play. The Atlantic City casinos are prevented by state regulators from offering machine games that can give the player an advantage. I know it sounds weird. I can't figure it out either. It has something to do with the legality of games of chance versus games of skill.

Maybe the weird part is the other side of the coin: that some casinos offer a few games that can be beaten like some of the video poker games, 10-7 Double Bonus, 9-5 Deuces Wild and Full Pay Joker Poker, in which the players can actually have the percentage on their side.

Perhaps they will soon fade away. On the other hand, maybe so many people will continue to play them so badly that the casinos will continue to find them profitable; in spite of the fact that the correct play will net a player an advantage from about 0.15% to 1.0%, even without taking the value of the comps into account.

Along with gambling itself, casino gambling tends to get a bad rap. This is generally not deserved. Compare casinos to racetrack pari-mutuels. Some casinos hold as little as 5% overall, when you count the comps. All racetrack pari-mutuels will eat your lunch.

Pari-mutuels act as a clearinghouse by taking in everyone's wager, taking out a prime cut of 15% to 25% for themselves and the government, and then splitting up the balance amongst the winners. It is hard to prevail against that kind of percentage. Actually, it is all but impossible.

Table 2-5				
Gambler's Ruin				
Assume 200 units to win 20 against various House Percentages				
Player's Bankroll	Win Target	House Percentage	Probability of Ruin	Average Number of Plays
200	20	-1%	0.6%	1866
200	20	-0.15%	6.6%	4000
200	20	0%	9.1%	4000
200	20	1%	33.4%	5343
200	20	2%	55.1%	5059
200	20	3%	66.9%	4459
200	20	4%	79.8%	3891
200	20	5%	86.5%	3406
200	20	8%	96.0%	2389
200	20	10%	98.2%	1960
200	20	15%	99.8%	1330
200	20	25%	99.996%	800

However, that is nothing compared to the Lottery. Most lotteries have a percentage of 50%. You stand as much chance of hitting the big one, with the lottery, as you do being struck by lightning while having sex during a snowstorm... twice.

Then, there is the old joke about the fellow who kneels down beside his bed every night and prays: "Dear God, please let me win the Lottery." This scene is repeated day after day, year after year and finally a voice booms down from above: "Help me out a little here. Buy a ticket."

Mathematicians will tell you that the odds of winning the lottery are about the same, whether you buy a ticket or not.

Ignoring the Big One, the total return on the smaller lottery wins is sometimes as little as 10%. That means that the vast majority of lottery players get back only ten cents out of every dollar wagered. You should look at the lottery as a voluntary tax on the mathematically retarded.

They tell a story about a cowboy would ride into town every payday and head for the local bar. He would stop and say: "Howdy." to the bartender, have one drink and head for the poker game in the back room. After a while, he would emerge broke and downcast, go out get on his horse and not be seen again for another month. When he would come into town again, the same scene would be repeated. One day, the bartender felt sorry for the cowboy, called him over, bought him a drink and said to him: "Don't you know that the poker game in the back room is crooked?" The cowboy downed his drink and said: "Yeah, I know it's crooked, but it's the only game in town."

It is inescapable that if you don't play, you can't win. But, do yourself a favor: If you are going to gamble, gamble at something that gives you a reasonable chance to come out ahead once and a while. It makes it a lot more fun. Even if the amount won is relatively small, most people like being winners. You will win more often with games that give you a better percentage.

As I mentioned earlier, most casinos keep a relatively small percentage. And just look at what they provide for that percentage: a safe, attractive environment, an honest game, free drinks and a variety of other comps. For this, they take a variable percentage, depending on which games you play and how well you play them.

But, never forget that casinos exist to make a profit. They are expert at luring you into making dumb moves. In addition to free booze, they provide all manner of interesting and attractive games with miscellaneous wagers that are little more than sucker bets.

When run properly, casinos make very handsome profits. Some say the only way to win is to own the casino. That is very, very close to the truth. It is, for the most part, because the casinos almost always have the percentage on their side.

The key words are "almost always". All it takes is a little knowledge, along with a mountain of self-discipline, to take the percentage away from the casino. The essential knowledge consists of knowing which games to play and how to play them.

Chapter 3 – The Good Games

Here is where you get the straight poop about the best games to play at the casinos. All of them (5 or so) have one thing in common: If you play them skillfully enough, you can have the best of the odds; that is, you can play with the Percentage in your favor. Do not quit your day job just yet though. About the best you will be able to do is to wring out maybe a 1% edge in your favor.

The beatable games are:

1. Blackjack (about a 1% Player Edge)
   and four varieties of Video Poker:
2. Full Pay Joker Poker (1%),
3. 9-5 Deuces Wild (0.76%),
4. 10-7 Double Bonus (0.17%), and
5. Loose Deuces (0.15%).

Even with a potential advantage, winning consistently is not easy. You really have to know what you are doing and then do it. Knowledge and skill are absolutely essential. In every circumstance, there is one and only one correct play. Expert play does not involve hunches or intuition. Trying to fake it will get you plucked.

Apparently, the games in which the player can gain the advantage all continue to exist on a limited basis for about the same reason: there are not many folks who a) know what they are doing, b) have enough self-discipline to always do it right, and c) have enough of a bankroll to not fall victim to Gambler's Ruin.

Now, let's get down to cases...

Blackjack

With Blackjack, although you can theoretically gain an edge of as much as 2% or so and most Blackjack book authors claim you should be able to obtain a 1% edge, averaging 0.5% under actual casino conditions is probably a more realistic figure. Besides skill, it depends on a couple of factors: first, what the house rules are on the particular table, and second, whether or not you can get away with counting cards.

There is good news and bad news on this last point, whether or not the casino will let you count. Some will and some won't. It is a mixed bag.

In Las Vegas, they publicly frown on card counters and "reserve the right to refuse service to anyone." If you win consistently, one of the pit bosses will sidle up to you and inform you "your action is a little too strong" and invite you to play a different game.

Atlantic City, on the other hand, has lost this battle in court. To offset the effect, the rules on the Atlantic City games are a little tougher - they stick to multiple deck Blackjack. Other places... other circumstances. Check them out before you make a commitment.

Several years back, there was a big flap about card counting. A professor of mathematics, one Dr. Thorp by name, showed that the effect of card removal from the deck affected the favorability of the succeeding hands. If more high cards, aces and ten counts, remained in the deck, the deck favored the player, and it was a good idea, on the average, to increase the size of the bet for the remainder of the deck. (Edward O. Thorp, Beat the Dealer)

A fellow by the name of Ken Uston put the card counting lessons into practice in the Atlantic City casinos soon after they opened, and scared the hell out of them. The casinos barred him. He sued, won, and sold a lot of books on how to play Blackjack. (Ken Uston, Million Dollar Blackjack)

The casinos finally figured out that all they had to do was to shuffle up before the deck was played out and they could keep their advantage. For a while, some casinos shuffled up before every deal. By using more decks; 2, 4, 6, or even 8 decks, and reshuffling before enough cards were dealt for the card count to matter much, they could kick ass and take names. As the books sales soared, the customers poured into the casinos putting their money, newly learned card counting skills, and unreasonable expectations on the Blackjack tables.

My God, how the money rolls in. The casinos are so busy kicking ass; they barely have enough time to take names. Recently, an industry report estimated that the average Blackjack table in Las Vegas was worth nearly $400,000 a year, with the average house drop being 10 to 15% of all money wagered.

Selling books on how to play Blackjack has been almost as profitable. Almost all the books on Blackjack show the house percentage to be so small as to be insignificant if you simply use the basic Blackjack strategy. Charts and tables for basic play are legion. Perhaps not surprisingly, they are pretty much the same. And, so the books say, if you use their specific methods to count cards and adjust your bet sizes according to their formulas, you can turn the percentage dramatically to your advantage and finally afford to quit your day-job.

Most pit bosses will tell you privately that if you know someone who thinks he can beat the casino and is willing to bet big money, the casino will send a limo to pick him up, put him on a chartered airplane, install him in a fancy suite, treat him like royalty and relieve him of the burden of his excess wealth. Every large casino has a staff of people who do just that.

The truth? Well, over the short term, a few thousand hands of Blackjack or so, anything can happen: Luck is fickle. But over the long haul, the House Percentage grinds up the average players like sausage. Insufficient bankrolls get the rest. Most Blackjack players, even those who play perfectly and count cards like a machine, are under capitalized and overly optimistic.

Even the best card counters in the world have to work like demons, never making mistakes, while watching their bankrolls bounce up and down like cosmic yo-yos. After thousands of hours of play, they can expect to see profits that nearly offset their expenses, at best winning at a rate of approximately one average bet every two hours, provided they don't hit a bad streak that wipes out their bankroll, or lose their grip on reality while watching idiots and drunks who don't have a clue constantly misplay their hands and still stack up short term wins.

Most people at the Blackjack tables haven't even taken the time to learn basic strategy and are incapable or unwilling to even consider the concept of counting cards. They come in with inadequate finances and exorbitant expectations, seemingly oblivious to the importance of having a sufficient bankroll and a modicum of skill. Almost always, they simply put their trust in luck.

Almost always, sooner or later, they lose. But, like bad golfers who hit one good shot out of a hundred, that one good shot keeps them coming back. The casinos will tell you that individually, most players don't play enough hands for the percentages to mean much to them. On the average though, the house percentage grinds out a steady profit, which keeps the owners, stockholders and casino management smiling.

How to Play Blackjack

If you already know how to play Blackjack, you may skip this part down to the Blackjack Etiquette section. There you should pay particular attention to the instructions about not squealing when you get a Blackjack.

The object of Blackjack is for the player to get a hand totaling more than the dealer's hand without going over a total of 21; where Aces count either 1 or 11, at the discretion of the player, face cards and 10's count 10 and the lower value cards count their face value.

Play begins by the dealer shuffling up the cards and having one of the players cut the pack. The dealer discards, or burns, one or more cards from the pack. Then, cards are dealt one at a time, starting with the player at the dealer's left until all have two cards. One of the dealer's cards will be placed face up.

Starting with the player on the dealer's left, each player will be allowed to take one or more cards until they are satisfied with their hand or until their hand totals more than 21, in which case they have "busted". This means that they lose immediately, must turn in their cards and are out of the game for the remainder of the round.

If the player's first two cards are a pair, the player is allowed to split the pair into two separate hands. By putting the cards, face up and side by side on the dealer's side of his/her wager and adding an additional wager beside the initial wager, he/she signals the dealer that he/she wishes to split and play two hands. When it is that player's turn, the dealer will place an additional card on the first card of the pair, which is then played as a separate hand. This is repeated for the second card of the pair.

In most casinos, players are also allowed the option of "doubling down". This appears, to an observer, to be similar to splitting a pair in that the player again places his/her cards face up on the dealer's side of his/her wager and adds an additional wager beside the initial wager. When it is that player's turn, the dealer will place one additional card face down on top of the player's cards.

Occasionally, the house rules will allow the player to surrender. This means the player may give up a bad hand and lose only one half of the original wager.

When all players are satisfied with their hands or have gone bust, the dealer turns up his/her face down card and plays the hand according to precisely defined house rules, with no options for the dealer regardless of the values of the player's hands.

If the players have all busted, the dealer merely displays his/her hole card and the round is over. Otherwise, the dealer will deal more cards, as necessary, to his/her hand until it totals 17 or more. If the dealer has an Ace and a Six, the hand is referred to as a "soft seventeen" since the Ace may be counted as either 1 or 11. On this hand, the house rules differ from game to game. In some cases, the dealer is required to stay, or stand, with a soft seventeen. In other cases, depending on the house rules, the dealer must hit, or draw another card, with a soft seventeen. The house rule, for this option, is usually printed on the table.

In some casinos, a single deck Blackjack game may be offered. In these games, the dealer holds the pack in his/her hand and deals the cards directly out of hand. With the double deck game, as the name implies, two decks are used. It is also usually dealt from the dealer's hand. With these games, the player's cards are usually dealt face down and the player is allowed to pick up the cards to examine them and play the hand.

With a pack consisting of more than two decks; sometimes four, six, or even eight decks; after the cards are shuffled and cut, they are placed in a box or holder that is usually called a "shoe". Cards are dealt from the open end of the shoe by the dealer sliding them, face down, out of the shoe to the players.

On multiple deck games, the player's cards are usually played face up. The players are not allowed to touch their cards. They indicate to the dealer how they wish to play their hands with a series of gestures: a "come here" motion if they wish another card or a "wave off" or "stop" motion if they wish to stand. Playing the hands face up is of no consequence since the dealer may not vary his/her play from the standard house rules regardless of the value of the player's hand.

Although Blackjack is basically a very simple game and the play of the cards appears to be quite casual, there are some formalities that must be observed in casino play.

Blackjack Etiquette

About table etiquette: it is not optional.

To cash in, sit down, wait until the dealer has cleared the table from the previous hand and has begun to shuffle up. Then, place the money you wish to convert into chips in front of the play spot that is directly in front of your seat. Don't try to hand your money to the dealer, he/she is not allowed to take anything directly out of your hand. Park your chips close to the rail directly in front of you.

If it is a multiple deck game, the dealer may offer you a colored plastic card. Do not put it in your pocket or throw it away. It is used to indicate the cut point on the pack. After the dealer is finished shuffling, he/she will place the pack in front of the player who has the colored card whose job it is to "cut the deck" by placing the colored card into the pack. It must not be placed very close to either end of the pack, within five cards or so.

If it is a single deck game, sometimes the cut is made by hand. The deck is placed in front of the player who is to "cut the deck" who then, with one hand only, should gently pick up more than about 5 cards and less than about 47 cards from the deck and place them gently beside the remaining cards.

The player should not pick up the entire deck and perform various manipulations with it. That tends to honk off the dealer, who is required to call the pit boss over and explain that the dork in the Hawaiian shirt screwed around with the cards. The pit boss and the dealer will then have to examine the deck, count the cards, glare at the offending player and ask him to cut out the crap.

To make a bet, place a number of chips - totaling at least the table minimum amount and not exceeding the table limit, usually indicated on a placard at the corner of the table - on the play spot directly in front of you. If you should bet more than one chip, stack them up. If you bet more than one denomination of chip at a time, place the smaller denominations on top of the larger. Wait for the dealer to deal all of the cards. Note the dealer's up card.

If you are playing a hand dealt game, pick up your cards with one hand and keep your other hand off the table. Do not bend the cards. Do not remove the cards from the space above the table. If you want to stand, carefully tuck one corner of your cards under your chips on the play spot. If you are playing a face up game make a "stop" or "no" gesture with your hand when it is your turn to play. Do not touch the chips.

If you want to hit, wait until it is your turn, and make a scratching motion toward you with your cards or make a "come here" gesture if you are playing a face up game. The dealer will place the additional card(s) on his side of your money. Do not touch them. If your hand goes over 21, gently lay your cards face up on top of the card(s) the dealer just gave you. When you have enough cards (without going over 21), tuck the corner of your original two cards under your money or with a face up game make a "stop" gesture. Do not touch either the chips on the play spot or the hit cards the dealer placed face up on his side of your chips.

If you want to double down or split, place your cards, face up, on the dealer's side of your wager. Do not touch the original wager on the play spot. Then, place an additional wager beside your original wager.

To play split hands you don't handle the cards after placing them on the dealer's side of your wager. Then, give hand signals just like you were playing a game being dealt from a shoe. Starting with the card(s) that make up the hand on your right, make a come here motion for a hit, and a wave off or stop motion for a stand.

If the cards you turned up were a pair and you intend to double down rather than split, when it comes your turn, hold up one finger and tell the dealer "One Card". When you have turned up any two cards other than a pair, the dealer will recognize that you want to double down and will give you one card face down. Leave it alone. You run the risk of bending it if you peek and you will probably slow up the game. It's not going to change.

If the dealer gives you a Blackjack (two cards totaling 21), immediately place the two cards face up on the dealer's side of your wager. Do not squeal, particularly if I happen to playing nearby. The dealer usually pays off Blackjacks first, at the rate of 1.5 to 1 rather than the customary one to one, and immediately collects those two cards, before dealing to the other players.

Wait until the hand is finished to pick up your winnings. Then, stack'em or rack'em. That is, either put them in a stack, arranged smallest to largest on the play spot to wager them on the next hand, or pile them up next to the rail in front of you.

To summarize the table etiquette: 1) One hand on the cards in a single deck game – don't touch the cards on a face up game; 2) Never ever bend the cards; 3) Don't touch the money until the hand is over; 4) then, Stack 'em or rack 'em.

Insurance

When the dealer's up card is an Ace, the dealer will pause the Blackjack game and then will call for Insurance. This is a separate bet the player can make that the dealer has a 10-spot card in the hole, which will give the dealer a Blackjack.

To take the bet, which means that you think the dealer has it; you place a bet equal to one-half your wager in the strip labeled *Insurance* on the dealer's side of your money. To not take the insurance bet, which is what you should normally do, just sit there.

The dealer will peek at the hole card and, if it makes a Blackjack, the dealer will immediately turn the hole card over, collect everybody's cards and original wager, and will pay-off the insurance bets at odds of 2 to 1. The net effect being that the additional insurance wager saved the original wager so that it works out to a push. If the dealer doesn't have a Blackjack, he/she will collect the insurance wagers and the game will proceed.

A little simple arithmetic makes it obvious that taking insurance is normally a bad bet. Only 16 out of the unseen 49 cards will give the dealer a Blackjack, 33 won't (33 to 16) and the house only pays 2 to 1 if the dealer has it.

Taking insurance when you have a Blackjack is also not a percentage play. That is, it costs you 0.01% over the long haul. However, you will not be there for that long of a haul and you probably need the money to tip the cocktail waitress.

Therefore, if the player has a Blackjack (which he immediately turned face up on the dealer's side of his money) when the dealer calls for insurance, the player should take the insurance bet; in this case by announcing in a resolute voice: "Even Money". This is a shorthand method of taking insurance. It saves pushing chips back and forth. The dealer will immediately collect the player's Blackjack cards and pay off the wager at even money before peeking at the hole card.

From time to time, you will hear people say that you should always insure a 20. Or, that since the dealer didn't have the Blackjack the last x number of times, it would be a good bet this time. They are wrong.

A side note: when you are counting cards and the card count is +2 or greater (minus the Aces with the High Low count), the odds generally favor taking insurance.

Blackjack General Information

It makes no difference which seat you choose, sometimes one will be luckier than another, but there is no significant difference. The first position, to the dealer's left, is called First Base and most new players will feel a little hurried playing that position. The last position is called Third Base and tends to attract more attention than the other positions because it is obvious that the card(s) the last player takes has a direct bearing on which card(s) the dealer gets.

It makes no significant difference whether or not the other players play their hands correctly or not. The player in front of you did not "take your card". He/she paid for it. One card of a particular denomination, even if you are counting cards, will seldom make a significant difference in the overall probabilities. Poor play on the part of the other players will help as often as it will hurt.

The dealer will win more than half the time against the best players, more often against others; that is, those who think they are smarter than thousands of mathematicians.

Basic Blackjack Strategy

The question of how to play your hand, whether to stand, hit, split or double is referred to as Blackjack strategy. For each specific pair of cards you are dealt, there is one and only one correct play, which depends on strongly on the dealer's up card, and to a significant extent, the identity of the cards that have been removed from the pack.

The correct play can be computed by comparing the relative probabilities of making a hand that will beat the dealer's probable hands to the probability of going bust. Properly programmed computing machines can do this with ease. Human beings can't.

If you are willing to neglect the effect on the probabilities that the identity of the cards that have been removed from the pack can make on the outcome, a Basic Blackjack strategy may be computed. This Basic Blackjack strategy may be represented as a set of rules, a chart or table that will give the most appropriate play for any two card hand as a function of the dealer's up card.

For the first round from a freshly shuffled deck, Basic Blackjack Strategy is very close to absolutely perfect play. It represents the best possible play for the specific set of conditions that are in effect on that particular table. These conditions include all of the different variations in House rules but the number of decks being used is usually key.

Other house rules, such as which cards the player may double down with, whether or not the player may double down after splitting and whether or not the dealer must hit a soft seventeen, also can influence the best play for a particular hand. Different strategies are applicable to each variation. The strategies are all very similar.

Blackjack has evolved into three main variations: Single Deck, Double Deck, and Multiple Deck (which covers 4 or more decks). With all three variations, usually the players may double down on any first two cards, and are allowed to split any pair.

With Single Deck Blackjack, the players are usually not allowed to double down after splitting (if allowed, it is a good deal for the players). With Multiple Deck Blackjack, the opposite is usually the case, the players are usually allowed to double down after splitting. With Double Deck games, it depends on the particular casino.

How many decks are best for the players? The answer is unequivocal: the house percentage is higher with more decks. That is why most of the big popular casinos on the Las Vegas Strip, all of the New Jersey casinos and most of the Indian casinos only play Multiple Deck Blackjack.

With a Single Deck game, it is usual practice for the dealer to hit a soft seventeen. With multiple deck games, the dealer is usually required to stand on a soft seventeen. On each game, the rule is normally printed on the felt table covering. The dealer has no choice. The house usually does what the mathematics say is in their best interest. That is, it improves their odds to hit a soft seventeen in a single deck game and to stand with a soft seventeen in a multiple deck game.

Here, we get down to the nitty-gritty. If you really intend to be a winner, you have to commit some stuff to memory. Learning Basic Blackjack Strategy for the first time is about the most difficult thing that will be required of you in order for you to become a reasonably consistent winner.

Do not vary from the Basic Strategy. Do not get tricky. Do not play hunches. Trust the percentages. The casinos do. If you need a 5 and the player just ahead of you has drawn one, do not chicken out and stand - hit anyway. If you always make the Book Play, you will be a better Blackjack player than 99.9% of the people you play with.

To facilitate learning the best play for the several varieties of Blackjack, sometimes the different strategies are blended together into a generic Basic Strategy that, more or less, gives the best play for any of the varieties. Then, exceptions to the generic Basic Strategy, which depend on the various house rules, may be learned separately.

Another tack is to learn any one of the specific Basic Strategies and then learn the differences between the variations. It is pretty much six of one and a half a dozen of the other.

The table or chart that shows the best play for a particular situation is commonly referred to as a "cheat sheet" or is called "The Book". Most cheat sheets are drawn so that the numbers across the top indicate the dealer's up card; the numbers along the left side indicate the players hand; Blank means to do nothing (stand), H means hit, D means double down, and Sp means split.

The Basic Strategy tables shown here, "The Book", are largely the result computer simulations over many millions

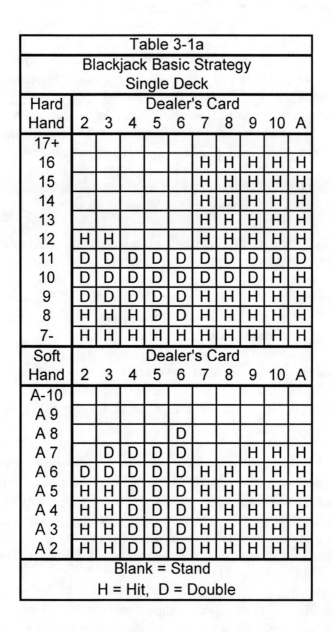

Table 3-1a									
Blackjack Basic Strategy Single Deck									
Hard Hand	Dealer's Card								
	2	3	4	5	6	7	8	9	10 A
17+									
16						H	H	H	H H
15						H	H	H	H H
14						H	H	H	H H
13						H	H	H	H H
12	H	H				H	H	H	H H
11	D	D	D	D	D	D	D	D	D D
10	D	D	D	D	D	D	D	D	H H
9	D	D	D	D	D	H	H	H	H H
8	H	H	H	D	D	H	H	H	H H
7-	H	H	H	H	H	H	H	H	H H
Soft Hand	Dealer's Card								
	2	3	4	5	6	7	8	9	10 A
A-10									
A 9									
A 8				D					
A 7		D	D	D	D			H	H H
A 6	D	D	D	D	D	H	H	H	H H
A 5	H	H	D	D	D	H	H	H	H H
A 4	H	H	D	D	D	H	H	H	H H
A 3	H	H	D	D	D	H	H	H	H H
A 2	H	H	D	D	D	H	H	H	H H
Blank = Stand									
H = Hit, D = Double									

Table 3-1b									
Blackjack Basic Strategy									
Single Deck - No Double After Split									

	Dealer's Card									
Pair	2	3	4	5	6	7	8	9	10	A
A	Sp	Sp	Sp	Sp	Sp	Sp	Sp	Sp	Sp	Sp
10										
9	Sp	Sp	Sp	Sp	Sp		Sp	Sp		
8	Sp	Sp	Sp	Sp	Sp	Sp	Sp	Sp	Sp	Sp
7	Sp	Sp	Sp	Sp	Sp	Sp	H	H	H	H
6	Sp	Sp	Sp	Sp	Sp	H	H	H	H	H
5	D	D	D	D	D	D	D	D	H	H
4	H	H	H	D	D	H	H	H	H	H
3	H	H	Sp	Sp	Sp	Sp	H	H	H	H
2	H	Sp	Sp	Sp	Sp	Sp	H	H	H	H

Single Deck - Double Allowed After Split										
	Dealer's Card									
Pair	2	3	4	5	6	7	8	9	10	A
A	Sp	Sp	Sp	Sp	Sp	Sp	Sp	Sp	Sp	Sp
10										
9	Sp	Sp	Sp	Sp	Sp		Sp	Sp		
8	Sp	Sp	Sp	Sp	Sp	Sp	Sp	Sp	Sp	Sp
7	Sp	Sp	Sp	Sp	Sp	Sp	Sp	H	H	H
6	Sp	Sp	Sp	Sp	Sp	Sp	H	H	H	H
5	D	D	D	D	D	D	D	D	H	H
4	H	H	Sp	Sp	Sp	Sp	H	H	H	H
3	Sp	Sp	Sp	Sp	Sp	Sp	H	H	H	H
2	Sp	Sp	Sp	Sp	Sp	Sp	H	H	H	H

Sp = Split

Table 3-2a									
Blackjack Basic Strategy Double Deck									
Hard Hand	Dealer's Card								
	2	3	4	5	6	7	8	9	10	A
17+										
16						H	H	H	H	H
15						H	H	H	H	H
14						H	H	H	H	H
13						H	H	H	H	H
12	H	H				H	H	H	H	H
11	D	D	D	D	D	D	D	D	D	D
10	D	D	D	D	D	D	D	D	H	H
9	D	D	D	D	D	H	H	H	H	H
8	H	H	H	H	H	H	H	H	H	H
7-	H	H	H	H	H	H	H	H	H	H
Soft Hand	Dealer's Card								
	2	3	4	5	6	7	8	9	10	A
A-10										
A 9										
A 8					D					
A 7		D	D	D	D			H	H	H
A 6	H	D	D	D	D	H	H	H	H	H
A 5	H	H	D	D	D	H	H	H	H	H
A 4	H	H	D	D	D	H	H	H	H	H
A 3	H	H	H	D	D	H	H	H	H	H
A 2	H	H	H	D	D	H	H	H	H	H
Blank = Stand H = Hit, D = Double									

Table 3-2b									
Blackjack Basic Strategy									
Double Deck - No Double After Split									
	Dealer's Card								
Pair	2	3	4	5	6	7	8	9	10	A
A	Sp	Sp	Sp	Sp	Sp	Sp	Sp	Sp	Sp	Sp
10										
9	Sp	Sp	Sp	Sp	Sp		Sp	Sp		
8	Sp	Sp	Sp	Sp	Sp	Sp	Sp	Sp	Sp	Sp
7	Sp	Sp	Sp	Sp	Sp	Sp	H	H	H	H
6	Sp	Sp	Sp	Sp	Sp	H	H	H	H	H
5	D	D	D	D	D	D	D	D	H	H
4	H	H	H	H	H	H	H	H	H	H
3	H	H	Sp	Sp	Sp	Sp	H	H	H	H
2	H	H	Sp	Sp	Sp	Sp	H	H	H	H
Double Deck - Double Allowed After Split									
	Dealer's Card								
Pair	2	3	4	5	6	7	8	9	10	A
A	Sp	Sp	Sp	Sp	Sp	Sp	Sp	Sp	Sp	Sp
10										
9	Sp	Sp	Sp	Sp	Sp		Sp	Sp		
8	Sp	Sp	Sp	Sp	Sp	Sp	Sp	Sp	Sp	Sp
7	Sp	Sp	Sp	Sp	Sp	Sp	H	H	H	H
6	Sp	Sp	Sp	Sp	Sp	H	H	H	H	H
5	D	D	D	D	D	D	D	D	H	H
4	H	H	Sp	Sp	Sp	H	H	H	H	H
3	Sp	Sp	Sp	Sp	Sp	Sp	H	H	H	H
2	Sp	Sp	Sp	Sp	Sp	Sp	H	H	H	H
Sp = Split									

Table 3-3a									
Blackjack Basic Strategy 4 to 8 Decks									
Hard	Dealer's Card								
Hand	2	3	4	5	6	7	8	9	10	A
17+									
16						H	H	H	H	H
15						H	H	H	H	H
14						H	H	H	H	H
13						H	H	H	H	H
12	H	H				H	H	H	H	H
11	D	D	D	D	D	D	D	D	D	H
10	D	D	D	D	D	D	D	D	H	H
9	H	D	D	D	D	H	H	H	H	H
8	H	H	H	H	H	H	H	H	H	H
7-	H	H	H	H	H	H	H	H	H	H
Soft	Dealer's Card								
Hand	2	3	4	5	6	7	8	9	10	A
A-10									
A 9									
A 8				D					
A 7		D	D	D	D			H	H	H
A 6	H	D	D	D	D	H	H	H	H	H
A 5	H	H	D	D	D	H	H	H	H	H
A 4	H	H	D	D	D	H	H	H	H	H
A 3	H	H	H	D	D	H	H	H	H	H
A 2	H	H	H	D	D	H	H	H	H	H
Blank = Stand H = Hit, D = Double									

Table 3-3b									
Blackjack Basic Strategy									
4 to 8 Decks - No Double After Split									
Dealer's Card									
Pair	2	3	4	5	6	7	8	9	10	A
A	Sp	Sp	Sp	Sp	Sp	Sp	Sp	Sp	Sp	Sp
10										
9	Sp	Sp	Sp	Sp	Sp		Sp	Sp		
8	Sp	Sp	Sp	Sp	Sp	Sp	Sp	Sp	Sp	Sp
7	Sp	Sp	Sp	Sp	Sp	Sp	H	H	H	H
6	H	Sp	Sp	Sp	Sp	H	H	H	H	H
5	D	D	D	D	D	D	D	D	H	H
4	H	H	H	H	H	H	H	H	H	H
3	H	H	Sp	Sp	Sp	Sp	H	H	H	H
2	H	H	Sp	Sp	Sp	Sp	H	H	H	H
4 to 8 Decks - Double Allowed After Split									
Dealer's Card									
Pair	2	3	4	5	6	7	8	9	10	A
A	Sp	Sp	Sp	Sp	Sp	Sp	Sp	Sp	Sp	Sp
10										
9	Sp	Sp	Sp	Sp	Sp		Sp	Sp		
8	Sp	Sp	Sp	Sp	Sp	Sp	Sp	Sp	Sp	Sp
7	Sp	Sp	Sp	Sp	Sp	Sp	H	H	H	H
6	Sp	Sp	Sp	Sp	Sp	Sp	H	H	H	H
5	D	D	D	D	D	D	D	D	H	H
4	H	H	H	Sp	Sp	H	H	H	H	H
3	Sp	Sp	Sp	Sp	Sp	Sp	H	H	H	H
2	Sp	Sp	Sp	Sp	Sp	Sp	H	H	H	H
Sp = Split									

of hands. They are not exact. They are, however, probably good enough for government work. Various sources show minor differences in Basic Strategy, which largely the result from whether the Basic Strategy was computed as a function of specific card combinations or as the result of computer simulation. The differences are mostly trivial.

You should memorize The Book even though most of the casinos will allow you to refer to a cheat sheet while you play. Knowing the correct play will reduce your stress level and allow you to enjoy the game.

As you look over the tables, you will see that it is fundamental to good Blackjack play that you particularly avoid the risk of going bust when the dealer's up-card is a six or less. Since the dealer will be required to hit, to take one or more cards when his up-card is a six or less, it is more likely that he might bust and make you an automatic winner regardless of the value of your hand.

The play rule is simple: If the dealer shows a six or less, don't take a card if a 10 would bust you. The only exception to this rule is: when you have a 12 and the dealer is showing a 2 or 3, you should hit one time.

The other frequent case is when the dealer's up card is a 7, 8, 9, 10 or Ace. Under these circumstances, you should not be satisfied with any hand that totals less than 17. Novice players tend to shrink from taking a hit when their hand totals 15 or 16, when the dealer's up card is 7 or larger. That is simply wrong. Ask any mathematician who knows shoe polish from that other stuff.

The best way to play hands which contain an Ace that may be counted as either a 1 or 11 or when to split pairs varies depending on the number of decks and whether or not the player may double down after splitting. You just have to learn it, case by case.

If Surrender is allowed, you should give up any 15 versus a dealer's 10 and 16, except a pair of 8's, versus a 9, 10 or Ace.

One of the best ways to learn The Book is to copy the charts, fold them neatly, put them in your pocket, go to your friendly neighborhood casino, find a likely looking Blackjack table, join in, whip out the appropriate page of The Book, clutch it one hand while you play with the other and consult it before every play.

The first time "a suit" (pit boss type) wanders past, point to one of the more suspicious looking plays on the chart and ask his opinion. Tell him you are just learning how to play and you would really value his opinion. He will probably avoid giving you any specific advice other than telling you that learning Basic Strategy is really a good idea. That should serve to keep the dealer from giving you any grief about slow playing. If any of the players should give you any crap, smile and ask how they think you should play this particular hand. While they are giving you their opinion(s), use the time to look up the correct play on the chart.

Note the few differences in the cheat sheets. With a single deck game you should always double down with eleven, even against an ace; the more decks that are used, the less favorable that becomes. When you are allowed to double down after splitting, it is more profitable to split more hands.

As far as the play is concerned, whether the dealer hits a soft seventeen makes very little difference. If he doesn't, don't hit an A-7 versus a dealer's Ace.

However, essential as it might be, Basic Blackjack Strategy isn't good enough, by itself, to allow you to take the edge from the casino. How well you can do just using Basic Blackjack Strategy depends on the various house rules in effect at the particular table.

With single deck Blackjack in Las Vegas, the theoretical House Percentage when using Basic Blackjack Strategy varies from about 0.01% to about to about 0.18% depending on things like whether you can double down after splitting. The limitations on doubling down in Reno, typically only with two card totals of 10 or 11, results in a House percentage of 0.3% to 0.4%. With multiple deck Blackjack, which is the variety of Blackjack most frequently encountered, the theoretical House Percentage when using Basic Blackjack Strategy varies from about 0.4% to about to about 0.7%

To gain the Percentage from the house, a little more than Basic Blackjack Strategy is required in the way of skill. Since the probability of whether the dealer or player might win the upcoming hand is somewhat dependent on the composition of the pack after some have been dealt, a little knowledge can go a long way.

Trying to take into account the effect of the identities of the cards that have been removed from the pack on the correct strategy is the subject of card counting. While effective, the various methods are not exact.

However, simply adjusting your wager depending on the amounts of high and low cards remaining in the pack can significantly alter the expectations. If you do it accurately enough and often enough you can gain the Percentage.

Card Counting

Card Counting is a method of accounting for the effect of having played specific cards from the deck. It is used to estimate the favorability of the remaining cards. Removing 10's and Aces from a deck favors the dealer. Removing small cards from a deck favors the player.

The casinos publicly frown on card counting; some Nevada casinos won't tolerate it. However, casinos love people with money who think they have a system. Good card counters (those who continue to play successfully) never admit to card counting or call attention to their knowledge. In Nevada, it is necessary for card counters to be somewhat tricky since the casinos are allowed to exclude anyone from the casino for any reason whatsoever.

There are numerous card counting systems. Some are a little better than others. For sizing your bet, none is much better than the simple High Low (or Hi-Lo) System. In spite of all the hoopla made about it, card counting can be really quite easy, depending on which card counting system you use.

Table 3-4

Card Counting Systems	Card Value for:									
	2	3	4	5	6	7	8	9	10	A
High Low (Hi-Lo)	1	1	1	1	1	0	0	0	-1	-1
HiOpt I	0	1	1	1	1	0	0	0	-1	0
HiOpt II	1	1	2	2	1	1	0	0	-2	0
Knock Out	1	1	1	1	1	1	0	0	-1	-1
Advanced Plus Minus	1	1	1	1	1	0	0	-1	-1	0
Revere Point Count	1	2	2	2	2	1	0	0	-2	-2
Thorp 10 Count	4	4	4	4	4	4	4	4	-9	-4
Unbalanced 10's	1	1	1	1	1	1	1	1	-2	1
Uston APC	1	2	2	3	2	2	1	-1	-3	0
Ultimate	5	6	8	11	6	4	0	-3	-7	-9

To use the High Low System:
>   1) Start at 0
>   2) Every time you see an Ace or 10, subtract 1 (-1)
>   3) Every time you see a 2 thru 6, add 1   (+1)
>   4) 7's, 8's and 9's count zero   (0)

This gives you what is called the Running Count. Dividing the Running Count by the number of decks remaining to be dealt will give you what is called the True Count.

For example, with three players at the table:
It is easier to see if you do it with cards:
(For round one, start with 0.)
Player 1:   6,   3,   10
>   (+1, +1, -1 = +1)

Player 2:   6,   7,   Q
>   (+1, 0,   -1 = 0)

Player 3:   10,   10
>   (-1,   -1   = -2)

Dealer: 4,   5,   8
>   (+1, +1, 0 = +2)

(Which all adds up to +1.)

(For round two, the starting count is +1.)
Player 1:   5,   5,   7
>   (+1, +1,   0 = +2)

Player 2:   9,   8
>   (0,   0,   = 0)

Player 3:   10,   J
>   (-1,   -1   = -2)

Dealer: Q,   4,   9
>   (-1, +1, 0 = 0)

(Which all still adds up to +1.)

So, after two rounds, the Running Count is +1 and since only about one half deck remains to be dealt, the true count is +2.

With a couple of hours practice, anyone with an IQ greater than his hat size and an attention span exceeding a microsecond can become an expert card counter.

On the first round, after a shuffle, the dealer has the edge (count is 0). On subsequent rounds, if the count is greater than +2, the player has the edge. Since the count is more frequently below +2, the dealer has a higher probability of winning more hands than the player. Then, the player must make larger wagers when the deck composition favors him to win in order to come out ahead. In my experience, the dealer wins about 48% of the hands, the player wins about 44% and about 8% or so are pushes.

For single deck Blackjack, dealer hits soft seventeen and no double after the split, the approximate Player Percentage as a function of the High Low Count, may be estimated by subtracting the initial House Percentage (call it half a percent, 0.5%) from half the count. All that is left is to bet as much as you can get away with (within the bounds of the Optimum Bet size) when the count is high and bet as little as the table minimum allows when the count is below +2.

According to my computer simulations, the overall Player Percentage at single deck Blackjack is only a shade under 1% when you ramp your bets as a function of the High Low card count from 1 to 5 units: 1 unit when the count is +1 or less, 2 units when the count is +2… to 5 units when the count is +5 or more. Computer simulations are one thing; actual practice is another. According to my experience, playing single deck Blackjack you will be doing well to make 0.5%.

Under the same conditions, double deck Blackjack is almost as good for the player, provided the house allows you to double down after you split. Similarly, four deck Blackjack can be marginally profitable at about 0.3%. Six deck Blackjack has a very small theoretical Player Percentage under these same conditions, and eight deck Blackjack has a small Percentage, about 0.1% in favor of the house.

To overcome the small or negative Percentage with multiple deck Blackjack, some people suggest ramping up the wager harder as a function of the count. That works; so does just betting a gob when the count is +2 or greater.

There's the rub. The casinos can always spot card counters because they invariably place a larger bet after many small cards (and few large cards) have been played from the pack.

You would be well advised to hunt down single or double deck games until you have the Basic Strategy down pat and have learned to count without even thinking about it. Single deck Blackjack yields two to five times the win rate of six deck Blackjack under the ideal conditions of computer simulation. For most people who can count and play reasonably well, in a casino setting, the difference is probably between winning and getting drubbed.

Keeping a side count of the Aces played can marginally improve the Player's Percentage. With the High Low card count, the Insurance Bet can become profitable when the count is adjusted for Aces. Other card counting systems, particularly those that count Aces as zero, have the player adjust the wager accordingly when the Ace count is light. It is best to keep bets at the minimum level when only one or no Aces are left in the pack, since most of the player's advantage is obtained from the one and a half payout value for getting a Blackjack,

Adjusting the Book Play as the count changes can marginally improve your percentage. But... varying your wager based on the count is worth about 2 times the value of varying your play. To achieve the best results you will probably want to use a counting scheme that is considerably more complicated than the simple High Low.

Although its betting correlation is as high as any other of the card counting systems, the High Low play adjustment correlation isn't particularly good without keeping a separate side count of the Aces and making appropriate adjustments. Trying to remember complex play variations under the distracting conditions of actual casino play will increase your chances of making errors. Even an occasional error will wipe the small advantage gained by play variations. It's best to stick to basics.

To give yourself the best odds and keep it simple: you should play only single deck Blackjack games. If there are no single deck games convenient to where you live, move.

However, if you are intent on playing Multiple Deck Blackjack and wish to have the percentage in your favor, you really have no choice but to go all the way and memorize Strategy number charts that show you how to shift the Basic Strategy for that particular game.

For those circumstances or if you intend to get really serious about playing Blackjack and mean to invest some real time and money, not just hobby stuff, then the information in this book isn't really precise enough for your purpose. I recommend you obtain a copy of Stanford

Wong's book, Professional Blackjack, and memorize it. Further, you should invest in some serious computer software, such as Stanford Wong's Professional Blackjack Analyzer and then practice, practice, practice.

No, Stanford Wong is not my brother-in-law. Although I have met the man and chatted with him, I am sure he wouldn't recognize me if I bit him. Along with his work, that of Peter Griffin (Theory of Blackjack) and Edward Thorp (The Mathematics of Gambling and Beat the Dealer) belong on the bookshelves of anyone who is even half way serious about playing Blackjack for fun and profit.

Blackjack Bankroll and Bet Size

Bear in mind that the casinos have an effective counter measure to card counting, and they are not employing it. All they have to do is shuffle up before every deal. A few casinos tried it back in the days of the big card counting scare, but their business fell off so badly, they could hardly afford to keep the tables open. After taking a deep breath, consulting their mathematicians and actually giving the players a shot at it, much to their relief, they found that the vast majority of would-be card counters were so wildly optimistic and under bankrolled they simply busted themselves out by not bringing enough ammunition.

Unit bet size relative to bankroll size is at least as important as counting. Being under bankrolled is a killer. If you over-bet your bankroll, it doesn't matter if you are the world's premier card counter. You won't last long enough for it to matter.

For example, if you are on a $5 minimum table and ramping your bets from $5 to $25 as a function of the card count: $5 for a count of +1 or less, $10 for a count of +2, $15 for a count of +3, $20 for a count of +4 and $25 for a count of +5 or greater; then, by backing out the Optimal Bet Size, your bankroll should be at least $5,000.

Given that with the High Low counting system, the Player Percentage may be approximated by taking one half the count minus the initial House Percentage, then, at all counts of zero and below, you are over-betting by definition; the Percentage is not in your favor. Half of all hands dealt have an effective count of zero or less. When the casino has an average advantage of 1%, such as they do with these counts, and you have a 1,000 unit bankroll, it is nearly a 100% mathematical certainty that you will be beaten within 100,000 hands. Granted that is about one year of playing full time, but the point is: you need a really big bankroll just to stay alive.

At a count of +1, the percentage is so close to even that you really are gambling. The Gambler's Ruin calculations are absolutely clear that the bigger the bankroll, the better.

At a count of +2, for a game that has an initial House Edge of 0.5%, your Percentage is about one half of +2 minus the House Edge of 0.5% equals 0.5%. Since the Optimal bet size is about 0.75 times the Player Percentage times the Player Bankroll and you are betting $10, your bankroll should be at least $2,667. At a count of +3… your bankroll should be at least $2,000. At a count of +4… your bankroll should be at least $1,778. At a count of +5… your bankroll should be at least $1,667.

Let's see now, backing out through those numbers… $1,667, $1,778, $2,000, $2,667, the bigger the better and really big just to stay alive. If that doesn't work out to a bankroll of at least $5,000 to play $5 Blackjack, then I'll kiss your monkey in Macy's window.

Avoiding Detection

If you are going to play in casinos that frown on card counting, you need a strategy or act or something to give you some cover and help you avoid detection. Spreading your Blackjack play among several casinos can help you avoid being picked off as a card counter, but it also dilutes your level of comps. If you can strike up a relationship with the pit bosses and dealers, so that they consider you to be one of their friendly regulars, the fact that you are counting seems to become unimportant to them, unless, of course, you make the mistake of calling attention to it.

When possible, it is best to play on a table that has a low minimum and high maximum. Low minimum tables tend to attract less attention from the pit bosses and from the eye in the sky. The greater the spread between the minimum bet and the table limit, the better is your potential for profit.

But, big bets always attract attention, more so on low minimum tables. On low minimum tables, the dealers are usually required to point out to the pit boss that a larger than normal bet has been placed by calling out: "Checks Play".

Occasionally putting up a larger bet on the first hand out of a freshly shuffled deck is one way to cover being a card counter. It is really not that bad a bet. According to Stanford Wong, on a single deck game, with his benchmark house rules, the win rate is 99.81% for the first hand out of the deck, a House Percentage of 0.19% (Stanford Wong, Professional Blackjack, Pi Yee Press, La Jolla, CA, p 288).

Playing a progressive betting system across the first hands in a Blackjack session can be amusing as well as being useful cover. You need to have a larger bankroll to do it, but if you pick one of the more conservative betting systems (see Chapter 6), there is no inherent mathematical disadvantage to playing the system. Just be sure to get on a table with good house rules that has a table minimum that is significantly lower than your Optimum Bet Size.

The way to do it sounds more complicated than it is. Each time the dealer has shuffled up, rather than always putting up a minimum bet, recall what the outcome was of the hand that followed the previous shuffle and play one of the more harmless systems. Ignore what just happened on the last hand from the deck and concentrate on making the sequence of first hands from the deck a separate game within the game. For the rest of the pack, bet the count.

The variation of initial bet sizes, by itself, will help give you cover as being a card counter. It can provide some satisfaction for those times when you have put up a larger bet on the first hand and then a bunch of big cards show up, leaving the rest of the hands from the deck with bad counts.

Since you should be on a table with a minimum lower than your average bet to be doing this, cutting back to the table minimum will tend to conserve your capital and your sanity. But be careful about fooling around with betting systems; you know you've had too much to drink when you find yourself taking any betting system seriously.

Although it is possible for a player to gain an advantage over the casino... if he can increase his wager enough when the count is in his favor, and do it enough times for the percentages to work, the variability in Blackjack is awesome.

Most Blackjack players, even good card counters, are ultimately losers simply because they fail to anticipate the fluctuations their bankroll will undergo.

How much can you expect to win? Put the fantasies away. Even though one player at the Mirage in 1995 ran a few hundred dollars into nearly $1.5 million before he lost it all back, the win rate is seldom that spectacular.

If you play often and well, over the long haul you might average winning one average wager every two hours. For a $5 game, with a $7.50 average wager, that works out to $3.75 an hour. Most players tip the dealers and cocktail waitress more than that.

Please note that coming out a little ahead, over the long term with a lot of ups and downs in the short term, beats the malarkey out of getting plucked. With the application of a little knowledge, a little skill, a lot of self discipline and a good sized bankroll, it is just possible that those marginal results can be pressed up to some real profit.

After reading everything I can get my hands on, running billions of hands on my computer, and playing at least 20 hours a week for several years, I think it just might be possible to make a modest living playing Blackjack... given some important conditions:

1. Single or double deck games with good house rules,
2. An adequate bankroll ($20,000 to $50,000),
3. The patience of a Zen High Master (with a leather butt),
4. Tolerant casino personnel (who don't mind if you win),
5. Luck (It ain't called gambling for nothing).

High Payback Video Poker

Nearly perfect play at Video Poker is essential to winning consistently. Even an occasional lapse will wipe out a small theoretical advantage. It appears as if the casinos sort of dangle the high theoretical Payback games out there as bait. They seem to be confident that the high complexity of perfect play will bring home the bacon for them. They are seldom wrong. But, if you concentrate on the Video Poker games one at a time, they are perhaps a little easier to learn than Blackjack, and you don't have to be tricky with the casino personnel.

The Video Poker games covered in this section are the best the casinos currently offer. Games that can yield over 100% return by the application of skillful play are not allowed in the Atlantic City casinos; so don't look for them. Various other jurisdictions may have a few of these "Full Pay" machines mixed in with their common garden-variety house machines. You just have to look for them.

In addition to the four Video Poker games that are covered here which have a theoretical Payback that exceeds 100% with expert play, there are a few other Video Poker games like 10-6 Jacks or Better, 9-7 Jacks or Better and Double Double Jackpot that also top 100% but they are so rare, they are hardly worth mentioning.

Check out the literature. Go to the Gambler's Book Shop at Charleston and 11th Street in Las Vegas. Talk to the helpful, friendly staff. Take their advice about what is current and which authors and volumes are worth the read. Get on their web site. While you are online, check in with the wizardofodds.com and the lasvegasadvisor.com. To stay current you need do a bit of research regularly.

The Payback on some other Video Poker games can exceed 100% if the amount on the progressive jackpot meter gets high enough, but most of those are covered in the next chapter. The games covered in this chapter can give you a mathematical advantage outright, without including the comps or any special conditions such as Double Jackpot Promotion Night etc.

If you should find yourself playing a house game without the possibility of some comp value, knock it off. Play something, somewhere, where the casino gives you some value for playing. Never forget that every little bit that adds to your side of the ledger tends to shift the odds a little more in your favor.

Casinos tend to rearrange their furniture and fixtures rather frequently. On occasion, they will lose some or all of their high Payback Video Poker machines in the shuffle. Unless their business falls off significantly, those games often stay lost. Not all casinos offer games for which the theoretical Payback can exceed 100%. If you should find yourself in one of those, your best strategy is to leave.

The big advantage of the video poker machines over the reel type slot machines, from the standpoint of the player, is that the house percentage can be determined from the pay table on the face of the machine. The gaming regulators will not allow the casinos to modify the random number mechanism that controls dealing the cards. That's cheating.

However, the casinos can, and do, set up payoff tables to make it look like the players are getting a good deal when they are not. Basically the house decreases one or more of the smaller payoffs, which accounts for a large percentage of the total payout, and increases one or more of the larger payoffs that contributes only a small percentage to the overall payout.

For example, a 10-4 variety of Deuces Wild, which only pays 94.9%, is often substituted for the full pay 9-6 Deuces Wild game, which pays 100.76%. With Deuces Wild, the payoff for 4 of a kind accounts for well over 30% of the total payout. Reducing the payoff, with five coins played, from 25 coins to 20 coins increases the House Percentage by about 6%. The increase in the payout for the straight flush is almost insignificant by comparison but it tends to mask the fact that the Payback percentage has been significantly lowered.

Using The Strategy Tables

Expert play consists of always holding the cards that statistically offer the best chance to maximize the payoff. For any group of 5 cards, there are 32 different choices of what to do: hold none, hold the 1st, hold the 2nd... etc.

By doing a 32 Way Analysis, every type of hand can be analyzed and the Expected Values for each choice computed. Ranking the choices in terms of their Expected Values results in a method for determining the best possible strategy for dealing with any group of five cards.

These Hand Ranking Tables, on Tables 3-5a and b through Tables 3-8a and b show which card combinations are better choices for you to hold than others, in terms of their mathematically best Expected Values (EV). That is, for any group of five cards, holding the set with the highest EV score will result in the highest payoff over the long haul. The tables are arranged in order of highest EV first, so you can tell at a glance which card combinations are better.

For example, when you examine the five cards you are dealt, you take a look at what kinds of combinations you have, like three of one suit: a 3 card straight; or perhaps a pair of 10's. Then you check the Hand Ranking Table to see which combination has the highest EV. The higher on the chart a combination is, the higher its EV is and the better it is to hold that combination.

In the interest of compactness on the Hand Ranking Tables, hands such as a 3 card partial Inside Straight Flush are sometimes abbreviated as a 3 card Str Fl 2 gaps. Partial Straight Flushes that are blocked on one end, such as an A, 2 and 3 are considered to be the same as a 3 card Str Fl with 2 gaps. It can take a while to get the hang of some of the abbreviations, but don't despair. With a little patience and actual practice of looking up hands on the charts, it will eventually become less confusing.

It is important to note that playing 5 coins per hand is almost invariably required in order for you to achieve the highest Payback Percentage. This is because the Payoff for the Royal Flush is usually 250 for 1 if less than 5 coins are played per hand and 800 for 1 if 5 coins are played.

Rather than play a 25¢ machine one quarter at a time, find the identical 5¢ machine and play five nickels at a time. You will be risking the same amount and getting the same return, except for the Royal Flush: you will get $200 rather than $62.50. By the same token, rather than play a $1 machine one dollar at a time, it is much better to find the identical 25¢ machine and play 5 coins. You will only be playing 25¢ more per hand, but if you hit a Royal Flush you will win $1,000 rather than $250. Few things in the casino can be more embarrassing than hitting a Royal Flush with only one coin in the machine.

There are a few machines that require more than 5 coins to qualify for the 800 for 1 Royal Flush payout. You should always pony up enough to qualify for the bonus or else you should play something else.

Multiplay machines are just like the single play machines, only it takes more money to play them. For the first few months they were in the casinos, a few that offered 100% Plus Percentage games were available. They seem to have evaporated. The ones left all seem to have a House Edge.

There is no such thing as a "similar pay table". In order to stand a decent chance at winning at Video Poker, you must select games that have the exact pay tables represented by the 5 coin Pay Table at the top of each of the Strategy Charts on Tables 3-5a and b through Tables 3-8a and b.

Just to preclude any misunderstanding about which game is which, the full Pay Tables are illustrated on Tables 3-5c through Tables 3-8c. The various Strategy Charts, Hand Ranking Tables, cheat sheets or whatever you wish to call them just don't apply to games that don't have the exact, same Pay Tables.

It cannot be overemphasized that following the best play tactics can make all the difference between ultimately winning and losing. On any particular draw, if you knew what was coming, you could surely make the best play, but since you don't, acting on hunches only serves to increase the House Percentage over the long haul. The best you can do is to trust that the Percentages will ultimately work. So far that strategy seems to be working for the casinos.

Table 3-5a

Joker Wild - Kings or Better			
5 Coin Pay Table			
Royal Flush	4700	Full House	35
5 of a Kind	1000	Flush	25
Wild Royal	500	Straight	15
Straight Flush	250	3 of a Kind	10
4 of a Kind	100	Two Pair/K or B	5
	101% PayBack		

Rank	Handtype	EV
	With Joker	
1	**5 of a Kind**	200.00
2	**5 card Royal Flush**	100.00
3	**5 card Straight Flush**	50.00
4	**4 of a Kind**	23.75
5	**4 card Royal Flush**	7.29
6	**Full House**	7.00
7	**4 card Straight Flush**	5.98
8	**5 card Flush**	5.00
9	**4 card Inside Straight Flush**	4.92
10	**3 of a Kind**	3.94
11	**5 card Straight**	3.00
12	**3 card Royal Flush with King**	2.04
13	**4 card Flush**	2.02
14	**3 card Royal Flush**	2.00
15	**3 card Straight Flush**	1.87
16	**3 card Inside Straight Flush 1 gap**	1.72
17	**Joker + Ace or King**	1.68
18	**3 card inside Straight Flush 2 gaps**	1.56
19	**4 card Straight**	1.54
20	**2 cards Joker + 6 7 8 or 9**	1.48
21	**2 cards Joker + 5 or 10**	1.48
22	**2 cards Joker + 4 or J**	1.44
23	**Joker - Draw Four**	1.42

Table 3-5b

Joker Wild - Kings or Better

Always Hold Joker
Always Play Five Coins
Hold Highest Ranked Combination

Rank	Handtype	EV
	Without Joker	
1	5 card Royal Flush	940.00
2	5 card Straight Flush	50.00
3	4 card Royal Flush	23.88
4	4 of a Kind	23.65
5	Full House	7.00
6	5 card Flush	5.00
7	4 card Straight Flush	4.23
8	3 of a Kind	3.94
9	4 card Inside Straight Flush	3.10
10	5 card Straight	3.00
11	Two Pair	1.63
12	3 card Royal Flush	1.56
13	High Pair (Aces or Kings)	1.40
14	4 card Flush	1.04
15	3 card Straight Flush	0.74
16	Low Pair	0.73
17	3 card Inside Straight Flush 1 gap	0.60
18	2 card Royal Ace and King	0.58
19	4 card Straight	0.58
20	3 card Inside Straight Flush 2 gaps	0.49
21	2 card Royal w/ Ace or King	0.49
22	2 High cards - Ace & King	0.45
23	1 High card - Ace or King	0.45
24	2 card Royal (no Ace or King)	0.37
25	Nothing - Draw Five	0.33

Table 3-6a

Deuces Wild 9-5			
5 Coin Pay Table			
Royal Flush	4000	4 of a Kind	25
Four Deuces	1000	Full House	15
Wild Royal	125	Flush	10
5 of a Kind	75	Straight	10
Straight Flush	45	3 of a Kind	5
100.76% PayBack			

Rank	Handtype	~ EV
	With no Deuces	
1	**5 card Royal Flush**	800.00
2	**4 card Royal Flush**	19.85
3	**5 card Straight Flush**	9.00
4	**4 of a Kind**	5.85
5	**5 card Full House**	3.00
6	**3 of a Kind**	2.02
7	**5 card Flush**	2.00
8	**5 card Straight**	2.00
9	**4 card Straight Flush**	1.66
10	**4 card Inside Straight Flush**	1.38
11	**3 card Royal Flush**	1.29
12	**1 Pair (never 2 Pair)**	0.56
13	**3 card Straight Flush**	0.52
14	**4 card Flush**	0.51
15	**4 card Straight**	0.51
16	**3 card Straight Flush 1 gap**	0.44
17	**2 card Jack - 10 Royal**	0.37
18	**3 card Straight Flush 2 gaps**	0.36
19	**4 card Inside Straight**	0.35
20	**2 card Queen High Royal**	0.34
21	**2 card K High Royal (K-Q, K-Q, K-J)**	0.33
22	**Nothing - Draw five**	0.33

Table 3-6b

Rank	Handtype	EV
Deuces Wild 9-5		
Always Hold Every Deuce		
Hold Highest Ranked Combination		
	With 3 Deuces	
1	**5 card Wild Royal**	25.00
2	**5 of a Kind (10s through Aces only)**	15.00
3	**3 Deuces**	15.00
	With 2 Deuces	
1	**5 card Wild Royal**	25.00
2	**5 of a Kind**	15.00
3	**5 card Straight Flush**	9.00
4	**4 of a Kind**	5.85
5	**4 card Wild Royal**	5.02
6	**4 card Straight Flush**	3.32
7	**2 Deuces**	3.27
	With 1 Deuce	
1	**5 card Wild Royal**	25.00
2	**5 of a Kind**	15.00
3	**4 card Straight Flush**	9.00
4	**4 of a Kind**	5.85
5	**4 card Wild Royal**	3.66
6	**5 card Full House**	3.00
7	**4 card Straight Flush**	2.21
8	**3 of a Kind**	2.02
9	**5 card Flush**	2.00
10	**5 card Straight**	2.00
11	**4 Card Straight Flush with 1gap**	1.94
12	**4 Card Straight Flush with 2gaps**	1.70
13	**3 card Wild Royal**	1.32
14	**3 card Straight Flush (7 high or higher)**	1.09
15	**1 Deuce**	1.03

Table 3-7a

Double Bonus Poker			
5 Coin Pay Table			
Royal Flush	4000	Full House	50
Straight Flush	250	Flush	35
Four Aces	800	Straight	25
Four 2s, 3s, 4s	400	3 of a Kind	15
Four 5s - Ks	125	Two Pair/JOB	5
100.17% PayBack			
Always Play Five Coins			
Hold Highest Ranked Combination			

Rank	Handtype	EV
1	5 card Royal Flush	800.00
2	4 of a Kind	65.38
3	5 card Straight Flush	50.00
4	4 card Royal Flush	18.95
5	Three Aces	10.11
6	Full House	10.00
7	5 card Flush	7.00
8	3 of a Kind	5.43
9	5 card Straight	5.00
10	4 card Straight Flush	3.70
11	4 card Inside Straight Flush	2.57
12	Two Pair	1.77
13	Pair Aces	1.76
14	High Pair	1.46
15	4 card Flush	1.45
16	3 card Royal Flush	4.43

Table 3-7b

	Double Bonus Poker	
	Always Play Five Coins	
	Hold Highest Ranked Combination	
Rank	**Handtype**	**EV**
17	4 card Straight	0.85
18	Pair 2s 3 or 4s	0.83
19	3 card Jack High Straight Flush	0.79
20	3 card Inside Str Fl - 2High Cards	0.78
21	Low Pair, 5s - 10s	0.74
22	4 card Ace High Straight	0.68
23	3 card Inside Str Fl -1 High Card	0.66
24	3 card Straight Flush	0.65
25	2 card Queen - Jack Royal	0.58
26	3 card Inside Straight Flush	0.58
27	3 card Flush - 2 High Cards	0.58
28	2 High Card Royal	0.55
29	3 cards: King Queen Jack	0.52
30	2 card Jack - 10 Royal	0.48
31	3 card inside Str Flush - 2 gaps	0.47
32	2 High Cards	0.47
33	3 card Flush - 1 High Card	0.46
34	1 Ace	0.46
35	2 card King or Queen - 10 Royal	0.45
36	1 High Card	0.44
37	4 card Inside Straight	0.43
38	3 card Flush	0.36
39	Nothing - Draw Five	0.33

Table 3-8a

Loose Deuces			
5 Coin Pay Table			
Royal Flush	4000	4 of a Kind	20
Four Deuces	2500	Full House	15
Wild Royal	125	Flush	10
5 of a Kind	75	Straight	10
Straight Flush	40	3 of a Kind	5
100.15% PayBack			

Rank	HandType	EV
	With no Deuces	
1	**5 card Royal Flush**	800.00
2	**4 card Royal Flush**	19.57
3	**5 card Straight Flush**	8.00
4	**4 of a Kind**	4.94
5	**5 card Full House**	3.00
6	**5 card Flush**	2.00
7	**5 card Straight**	2.00
8	**4 card Straight Flush**	1.53
9	**3 of a Kind**	1.82
10	**3 card Royal Flush**	1.35
11	**4 card Inside Straight Flush**	1.28
12	**3 card Ace High Royal**	1.27
13	**1 Pair (never 2 Pair)**	0.52
14	**4 card Flush**	0.51
15	**4 card Straight**	0.51
16	**3 card Straight Flush**	0.48
17	**3 card Straight Flush 1 gap**	0.47
18	**2 card Jack - 10 Royal**	0.37
19	**3 card Straight Flush 2 gaps**	0.34
20	**4 card Inside Straight**	0.34
21	**2 card Queen High Royal**	0.34
22	**Nothing - Draw five**	0.32

Table 3-8b

Rank	HandType	EV	
	Loose Deuces		
	Always Play 5 Coins		
	Always Hold Every Deuce		
	Hold Highest Ranked Combination		
Rank	**HandType**	**EV**	
	With 3 Deuces		
1	**3 Deuces**	26.85	
	With 2 Deuces		
1	**5 card Wild Royal**	25.00	
2	**5 of a Kind**	15.00	
3	**5 card Straight Flush**	8.00	
4	**4 of a Kind**	4.94	
5	**4 card Wild Royal**	4.47	
6	**2 Deuces**	3.60	
	With 1 Deuce		
1	**5 card Wild Royal**	25.00	
2	**5 of a Kind**	15.00	
3	**5 card Straight Flush**	8.00	
4	**4 of a Kind**	4.94	
5	**4 card Wild Royal**	3.66	
6	**5 card Full House**	3.00	
7	**4 card Straight Flush**	2.11	
8	**5 card Flush**	2.00	
9	**5 card Straight**	2.00	
10	**4 Card Sraight Flush with 1gap**	1.85	
11	**3 of a Kind**	1.82	
12	**4 Card Sraight Flush with 2gaps**	1.60	
13	**3 card Wild Royal**	1.30	
14	**1 Deuce**	1.04	

Joker Wild Video Poker

As with all video poker games, you must be absolutely certain that you are playing the right machine. The pay tables are not always prominently displayed and one minor difference can make all the difference between a plum and a lemon. The pay table for the Full Pay Joker Wild Video Poker game that pays 101% is shown on Table 3-5c.

Table 3-5c

Joker Wild Video Poker Pay Table				
101% Payback with 4700 Royal				
100.65% Payback with 4000 Royal				
	1 Coin	2 Coins	3 Coins	4 Coins	5 Coins
Royal Flush	250	500	750	1000	4700
5 of a Kind	200	400	600	800	1000
Wild Royal	100	200	300	400	500
Straight Flush	50	100	150	200	250
4 of a Kind	20	40	60	80	100
Full House	7	14	21	28	35
Flush	5	10	15	20	25
Straight	3	6	9	12	15
3 of a Kind	2	4	6	8	10
Two Pair	1	2	3	4	5
Kings or Better	1	2	3	4	5

The 5 coin Pay Table, for this Full Pay Joker Poker game is also shown on the Hand Ranking Tables, Tables 3-5a and 3-5b, which outline the best play strategy.

Joker Wild, Kings or Better, is an extremely volatile game. If you don't hit Four of a Kind regularly, it can be brutal. The payout for Four of a Kind of 20 for 1 is very significant with this Joker Wild game and largely accounts for its high volatility. The payout for Five of a Kind, at 200 for 1, is analogous to the 4 Deuces payout in Deuces Wild.

The best play depends on whether the hand contains a wild card. Under no circumstance should the Joker ever be discarded. Should you ever find yourself throwing away the Joker from a Wild Royal, you should immediately order some coffee or go sleep it off.

Even when the hand appears to contain little of value but the Joker, you should hold something to go with it. Take a look at Table 3-5a, lines 20, 21 and 22; it is pretty difficult to catch a hand that doesn't require holding something. It seems to come down to a hand which contains an unsuited 2, 3, Queen and a Phantom. Somewhat surprisingly, the middle-sized cards are theoretically preferable to holding a 10 or Jack with the Joker.

With no Joker, Two Pair is a pretty good hand and should always be held, never broken up (Table 3-5b, line 11). Even if one of the pair is Aces or Kings, the low pair should not be discarded.

Always be on the lookout when your hand contains 3 cards of the same suit. If they can be filled in to make a Straight Flush, they are a viable hold (Table 3-5b, lines 17 and 20). Without having to count on your fingers, subtract the value of the bottom card from the top. If it equals 4 or less, yes.

You should be careful not to hold unsuited Queens and Jacks since, unlike the Jacks or Better games, they are of no special value in this game.

With a 4,000 coin Royal Flush Jackpot and expert play the Payback percentage is 100.65%. With 4,700 coins, it is 101%. The best play for these variations is identical.

Deuces Wild Video Poker

Deuces Wild Video Poker, 9-5 Full Pay, in which all four deuces are wild, is considerably different from the other games. The 9-5 designation refers to the payoff for a Straight Flush of 9 for 1 and for Four of a Kind of 5 for 1. This shorthand designation is used for simplicity. Be sure to check all of the payouts on the pay table against the chart shown on Table 3-6c. The machine manufacturers and casinos really do try to get tricky

Table 3-6c

Deuces Wild Video Poker Pay Table 100.76% Payback					
	1 Coin	2 Coins	3 Coins	4 Coins	5 Coins
Royal Flush	250	500	750	1000	4000
Four Deuces	200	400	600	800	1000
Wild Royal	25	50	75	100	125
5 of a Kind	15	30	45	60	75
Straight Flush	9	18	27	36	45
4 of a Kind	5	10	15	20	25
Full House	3	6	9	12	15
Flush	2	4	6	8	10
Straight	2	4	6	8	10
3 of a Kind	1	2	3	4	5

The best play tactics, as shown on Tables 3-6a and 3-6b, depend on the number of Deuces in the hand. With fewer Deuces the best play tactics become increasing more complicated. There are no circumstances that justify discarding a deuce, not even when you hold a Wild Royal with a single Deuce.

With three Deuces, the only 5 card hands that should be held are a Wild Royal (do not chuck the two suited face cards – it isn't worth the gamble) or a Five of a Kind that consists of the three Deuces and a pair that are 10's or larger. The value of a Wild Royal and the possibility of getting one together with the value of possibly drawing the fourth Deuce makes it worth your while to throw away any small pair that forms 5 of a Kind with a three Deuce Hand.

Five of a Kind with a two Deuce hand is another matter; you should always hold it. In addition to holding a 5 card Straight Flush with two Deuces, you should always hold any pair which with the two Deuces makes Four of a Kind. The weakest hand you should hold with two Deuces is a four card Straight Flush. You should break up all Straights and Flushes and just hold the two Deuces.

With only one Deuce, Straights and Flushes are worth holding as they are with no Deuces, but Two Pair should not be held. It is best to hold only one Pair, and discard the other. It doesn't matter which you choose; chuck one pair.

Some of the play choices are very close with Deuces Wild. For example, the 2 card King High Royals, shown on line 21 of Table 3-6a, should be held only if there are no other cards of that suit in the hand. Note that you should not hold a 2 card Ace High Royal Flush.

All things considered: the high Payback, the relatively uncomplicated strategy, ease of learning… etc; the Full Pay, 9-5 Deuces Wild may just be the best choice of all Video Poker games. Up until this point in time, the Full Pay Deuces Wild machines have been widely available in the Las Vegas casinos, at least in the 25¢ denomination.

With expert play the Payback percentage for Full Pay Deuces Wild is 100.76%. With just a little practice, almost anyone can become an expert at Deuces Wild.

Double Bonus Video Poker

The 10-7 Double Bonus Poker, as shown by the pay table on Table 5-7c, is similar to the older Bonus Poker game but it pays twice as much for Four Aces, Twos, Threes, and Fours. The catch is that it only pays 1 for 1 for Two Pair. The 1 for 1 payoff for Two Pair largely offsets the higher bonus payoff.

Table 3-7c

Double Bonus Video Poker Pay Table				
100.17% Payback				
	1 Coin	2 Coins	3 Coins	4 Coins	5 Coins
Royal Flush	250	500	750	1000	4000
Four Aces	160	320	480	640	800
Four 2s, 3s, or 4s	80	160	240	320	400
Four 5s thru Ks	50	100	150	200	250
Straight Flush	50	100	150	200	250
Full House	10	20	30	40	50
Flush	7	14	21	28	35
Straight	5	10	15	20	25
3 of a Kind	3	6	9	12	15
Two Pair	1	2	3	4	5
Jacks or Better	1	2	3	4	5

However, a very small Player Percentage of 0.17% may be squeezed out with very sharp play. The complexity of the best play probably accounts for this game being the most widely available of all the Full Pay games.

For this variation, the high value of four Aces justifies discarding the Low Pair from a Full House containing three Aces (Table 3-7a, lines 5 and 6). This does not also apply to Two Pair with Two Aces; you should hold the Two Pair (Table 3-7a, lines 12 and 13).

Perhaps the most difficult hold is to ignore the Three card Royal when you have Four to a Flush. You should give up the shot at the Royal Flush and take the one card draw to a regular Flush (Table 3-7a, lines 15 and 16).

Almost as difficult is to keep the High Pair when you also have Three to a Royal. All high pairs outrank three to a royal (Table 3-7a, lines 14 and 16).

Due to the bonus value of the Four of a Kinds, a pair of 2s, 3s, or 4s outranks a four card straight which outranks any other low pair.

With Double Bonus Video Poker, holding a 4 card inside straight is somewhat better than drawing 5 cards.

There are many minor additions and exceptions to the plays shown on Table 3-7 because of "interferences" from the discards and as a result, the plays shown on Table 3-7 are only approximate. You might lose 0.07% as a result.

To really achieve an expert level of play with Double Bonus Video Poker you need to obtain one of the better software programs and practice furiously. Many of the plays are difficult to commit to memory because they just don't feel right when you are used to playing other games.

With expert play the Payback percentage is 100.17%. The time and energy spent in learning the intricacies of this game to achieve such a small percentage are difficult to justify if the better games such as 9-5 Deuces Wild or Full Pay Joker Poker are available. With a 25¢ machine, you might make as much as $1.05 an hour, on the average.

Loose Deuces Video Poker

The attraction of the Loose Deuces Video Poker game illustrated by the pay table on Table 3-8a is that it pays 2,500 coins for Four Deuces with 5 coins played, which is two and a half times that of the regular Deuces Wild. However, this increase is more than offset by the lower payout on Four of a Kind of 4 for 1 rather than 5 for 1.

Table 3-8c

Loose Deuces Video Poker Pay Table 100.15% Payback					
	1 Coin	2 Coins	3 Coins	4 Coins	5 Coins
Royal Flush	250	500	750	1000	4000
Four Deuces	500	1000	1500	2000	2500
Wild Royal	25	50	75	100	125
5 of a Kind	15	30	45	60	75
Straight Flush	8	16	24	32	40
4 of a Kind	4	8	12	16	20
Full House	3	6	9	12	15
Flush	2	4	6	8	10
Straight	2	4	6	8	10
3 of a Kind	1	2	3	4	5

Not surprisingly, the best play strategy is shifted somewhat toward capitalizing on the higher Deuces payout. With Three Deuces in a hand, only the Deuces should be held. Even a Wild Royal is of lesser value than the possibility of drawing the fourth Deuce. With Two Deuces, you should not hold four cards to a straight flush.

For hands that contain one Deuce, the play is very similar to the regular Deuces wild except that Three of a Kind out-ranks a Four Card Straight Flush with 2 Gaps (such as a 10, 9, 6 and a deuce – which is the same as 1 Gap when it is also blocked at the low end by being smaller than 7 high).

The best play for hands containing no deuces is virtually identical to that of the regular Deuces Wild with the exception that values of the partial Straight flushes are reduced somewhat.

Although it is a lot of fun to hit the Four Deuces with the generous payout of 500 for 1, the loss of more than a half a percentage point, from that of the Full Pay 9-5 Deuces Wild makes playing this game questionable when the full pay version is available.

Also, the differences between the best play strategies for the two games may be just enough to throw you off your best game with the 9-5 version if you aren't really careful.

With expert play, the maximum Payback that can be achieved with Loose Deuces is 100.15%. You would be well advised to stick with the Full Pay Deuces Wild.

Other High Pay Video Poker Games

There are, of course, other varieties of Video Poker for which the theoretical best play can yield a Payback that can exceed 100%.

From time to time you might run across a 9-7 Jacks or Better (100.8% Payback) or a 10-6 Jacks or Better (100.7% Payback). The best play for both of these games is close enough to the best play with the standard 9-6 Jacks or Better (99.5% Payback) that you may comfortably use the best play strategy for the standard 9-6 version which is shown in the next chapter.

Occasionally an odd game will show up that appears to be favorable to the player. Don't trust that you can guess the correct play. It is often counter intuitive. Video Poker software is readily available that can analyze the game, calculate the % Payback and drill you on the best play. The software packages are inexpensive, ranging from $20 to $150, and are worth every penny.

It is surprising just how much of a bankroll it takes to play the Video Poker games. The risk of ruin is quite high, even with the best games. To have a reasonable chance of never being wiped out you need to have total reserves on the order of 2,500 to 5,000 units, where a unit is the full amount you play on each hand.

Playing with a small bankroll will get you wiped out from time to time, but with the games that you can play well enough to have the Percentage in your favor, there is no reason you shouldn't take another whack at it, when you can afford it. Unless you are misplaying the hands, sooner or later you will beat the little rascals.

If you restrict your play to those games that have a Payback greater than 100% and play them reasonably well, you can play them with impunity and with the certain knowledge that you will eventually come out ahead.

Chapter 4 - The Bad Games

By naming this chapter The Bad Games, do I really mean to tell you that all of the games covered here shouldn't be played if you want to win? Yup, if you play them long enough, no matter how well you play them, you will lose.

Generally, this group of games: Baccarat, Craps, Pai Gow, High Payback Slots and Medium Payback Video Poker; are sprinkled liberally throughout the casino, flanked by a host of sucker games. Hidden amongst them, if they are there at all, will be the few good games, Blackjack and the High Payback Video Poker varieties, mentioned in the last chapter. Only if you cannot find one of the good games should you even consider playing these.

All of these games, including Craps and James Bond's personal favorite Baccarat, mathematically favor the house. Even though the House Percentages are not exorbitant, they will grind you down. Anyone who tells you that there is some tricky way of playing or betting these games that will make you a sure winner is either a liar, a charlatan or a fool. If that offends anyone and they want to make something out of it, I recommend they take it up with Mike Tyson. Talk about bad odds...

There are only a couple of valid reasons to play these games: 1. The casino is offering such a strong promotional inducement that it would be like giving away money not to play, and 2. You have already won so much money that you are feeling sorry for the casino and would like to give some of it back.

In order to be susceptible to reason number 1, the House Percentage has to be reasonably small. When the House

Percentage is under about 2%, the further under the better, this group of casino games can be quite playable, but only under the condition that the inducements, cash back and comps, offset the House Percentage.

When the House Percentage on the game in question begins to approach or exceed 2%, I tend to put the game in another category. It shifts from bad to ugly and no inducements are strong enough to make it embraceable.

Comps Can Make Them Playable

The comps, complimentaries, the free goodies that the casinos give to induce people to play, are not to be sneered at. Depending on your level of play, you might be given anything from a free drink, a breakfast buffet, dinner for two, show tickets, free lodging, limousine service, air fare... All just for playing, win or lose. The more you play, the more you get.

Of course the casino expects you to lose. That's why they are doing it: for the money. However, they are actually willing to give you back some of the money they expect you to lose, whether you lose it or not. Now, if you play the games very well, that can be a very good deal. You don't even have to win to come out ahead. If you just break even, you can get your expenses paid for.

Even with the bad games, skill plays a significant role. If you don't play well, the cost can be very high. If you play perfectly, sometimes you may win, but more often you will lose. How often you do which, depends on the percentage. With the good games, if you play well, you will win more often than you lose. With the bad games, even with perfect play and no fooling around, you will not quite break even over the long haul. With the ugly games, you don't stand a snowball's chance. The comps just tend to offset the cost.

If you are going to gamble, I can't think of a valid reason not to take the comps. They have value. They are easy to get. All you have to do is check with the casino host or with the casino player's club. They will make the arrangements for you to be "rewarded" for your play.

Some people have the attitude: "I'm not going to play enough to make it worth the effort to identify myself and give up some of my privacy."

Give me a break. It's not like you are not already on every mailing list out there anyway. Every merchant you deal with tells the credit companies everything they know about you. The credit companies sell you out every day, so does your bank, the state driver's license bureaus and the federal government. None of them are willing to buy your lunch.

If you are going to gamble for small stakes, you should get a player's card from the casino. Whenever you play a machine, you stick the card into the slot and it will automatically record your "play action". When you play one of the table games, give your card to the dealer or pit boss and your play will be tracked. All this does is to give the casino a basis for determining how much of a "reward" you should get. Usually it doesn't take much play action to get a free buffet. It varies a bit from one casino to another. Hey, a little something is better than a lot of nothing.

The player's club cards usually work on the basis of "points". For every dollar you wager, you accumulate say one point and then you may use your points to "purchase" food, beverages, lodging or merchandise at the casino's retail establishments. Some casinos will allow you to redeem your points for cash back. Cash back for player's club points is often 0.25%, normally ranging between 0.1% and 0.5%. If you run up $1,000 in play action, win or lose, you get maybe $2.50 cash back

You need to understand that the $1,000 play action doesn't necessarily represent $1,000 from your bankroll. It can represent very little real money. For example, sometimes you can play Video Poker all day, say 8 hours, on an initial investment as little as $20, get back your $20 along with some of the casino's money and the casino will "reward" you for playing. At Video Poker, on a 25¢ machine, you play 5 coins at a time for $1.25 a hand; at a rate of about 500 hands per hour... that works out to $5,000 in play action a day. The resulting comp value is not insignificant.

If you plan on playing for serious money, you should check in with the casino host. You can find out how much in the way of comps you can expect for your level of play action. You don't normally get the comps up front. You have to "earn" them and then you have to ask for them. That's not a big price to pay if you are going to gamble there anyway.

To find out what you can get for the amount you have to gamble, just go to the Player's Club booth or check with the Casino Host. They will be happy to tell you.

The comp policy for table games at the Stardust Casino in Las Vegas is about average for the established casinos. The criteria on Table 4-1 (stardustlv.com, August, 2004) are just a guideline and will vary depending on a number of factors including which games you play and how much the pit boss thinks your style of play is worth to the casino.

They try not to give back more than about 40% of what they think they should be able to beat you out of.

Table 4-1

Stardust Casino's Comp Criteria Chart for Table Game Play		
Average Bet	Hours	Complimentaries Extended
$15	4	Casino Rate
$25	4	Room Only
$50	4	Room and limited food and beverage
$100	4	Room, food and beverage
$125	4	One bedroom suite, food and beverage
$175	4	Two bedroom suite, food and beverage

Just for being a member of the casino's players club and being on their mailing list, the casinos will usually send you special offers from time to time. If you take advantage of them judiciously, the special offers can add significantly to your percentage. It will seldom add more than about 1% to the player's side of the ledger, but it can be enough to make the difference between a net win and a net loss.

For some of the Video Poker games that pay nearly 100%, the comps, the cash back programs in particular, can make them player's games rather than house games. The level of comps is usually the same whether a particular Video Poker machine has a payback percentage as high as 101% or as low as 90%. It's your choice.

You should never wonder why the casinos offer the various complimentary inducements: they do it for the money. It should go without saying that you shouldn't gamble away more money than the value of the comps that you expect to get, but you should always be aware of the comp value of your play. Comps are an integral part of casino gambling. Don't play without them.

Baccarat

There is an air of mystery about Baccarat. I find the game just a little strange somehow. It is quite simple to play.

None of the action is between the players at the table. Everyone plays against the house. Even though the shoe from which the cards are dealt passes from one player to another, it is just a formality. The dealer supervises the play and makes sure the correct procedures are followed.

The play of the cards is strictly according to formula. There are no discretionary plays. There is absolutely no skill involved whatsoever.

Cards are dealt to form two hands: a (hypothetical) Player's Hand and a Banker's Hand. After a few cards are dealt, one hand is declared the winner. The bets of those who bet against it are collected and those who bet on it are paid off.

Once I overheard a bystander ask another to explain how the game was played. The response was clear and correct: "Well, you put some money in one of those areas on the cloth that says 'Player', 'Banker' or 'Tie' and when they take it away you put some more money out there."

You can bet on the Banker's hand, which wins 45.9% of the time, is paid even money (minus a 5% commission) and has a House Percentage of 1.06%. You can bet on the Player's Hand, which wins 44.6% of the time, is paid even money and has a House Percentage of 1.24%. Or, if you are completely brain dead, you can bet that there will be a Tie, which occurs 9.5% of the time is paid 8 to 1 and has a House Percentage of 14.4%. If the Tie is paid at 9 to 1 the House Percentage is 4.8%; still lousy by any measure.

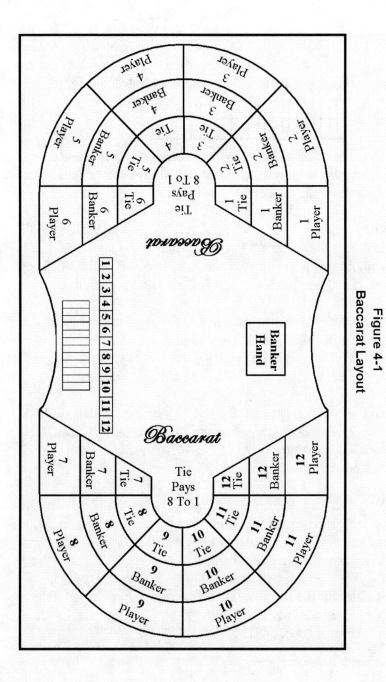

Figure 4-1
Baccarat Layout

If you bet on the Banker's hand and win, you have to pay a 5% commission (which accounts for the House Percentage of 1.06%) for each win sometime before you leave the table. They are quite casual about it, but don't forget that you owe it to them. There is no commission on wins with either the Player's hand or Ties.

There are two varieties of Baccarat played in the casinos. One is the large formal game played on a big table that can accommodate a dozen or so players and is attended by dealers in tuxedos or evening gowns. The minimum bet is usually $25 or more. A $100 minimum is not uncommon. The less formal game is usually played on a smaller table, without much hoopla, for stakes as low as $5 a hand. They are exactly the same in terms of odds and probabilities.

Supposedly Baccarat was invented a few hundred years ago for a King of France who wasn't considered to be very bright. The game is vaguely similar to Blackjack, but with the object being a score of 9 rather than a score of 21.

Of the two hands dealt, the one closest to 9 wins. 10's and face cards count zero and the other cards all count their spot value. If the points add up to 10 or more, the first digit is ignored: 11 is 1, 12 is 2, 13 is 3… etc.

Two cards are dealt to each hand. Depending on the value of the hands, more cards may or may not be drawn. One imagines that the choice was initially up to the King, but nowadays the rules are fixed.

If either of the hands totals 8 or 9, the game is over and the biggest wins. If not, and the Player's Hand totals 5 or less, it is dealt another card.

The Banker's Hand is then considered. If the Player's Hand did not take a third card, the Banker's Hand is not dealt a third card unless its total is 5 or less.

If the Player's Hand did take a third card, whether the Dealer's Hand takes a third card depends on the value of the Dealer's Hand and the third card dealt to the Player's Hand. If the Dealer's Hand is 3 or less, the Dealer's Hand takes another card, except with a total of 3 when the Player's third card was an 8. If the Dealer's Hand totals 4, then it is dealt another card if the Player's third card was a 2 through 7. If the Dealer's hand totals 5, it is dealt another card if the Player's third card was a 4 through 7. If the Dealer's Hand totals 6, it is dealt another card if the Player's third card was a 6 or 7. If the Dealer's hand totals 7, it is all over. Again, whichever hand is biggest wins, excluding the first digit of the total if the total is over 9.

You really don't need to remember any of the play rules. If you win, they will tell you. If you don't, they will take your money. It is a lot like tossing a coin; a lumpy coin maybe, one that sometimes lands on its edge so there can be a Tie. You can bet on Heads, Tails or Tie. It's best to not bet on the Tie with its 14.4% House Edge. Otherwise, it is just sort of a random walk kind of game. Sometimes you win; a little more often you lose.

That brings up the one aspect of Baccarat that has some merit. Since it is sort of a coin toss, as long as you remember not to bet on the Tie, there is never anyone who is playing any better than you. It doesn't matter how spacey you are or how drunk you get, as long as you stay off the Tie bet, you get the same House Percentage as any of the other players. You just can't be the worst player. Everyone is equal with regard to skill since none is required.

However, some players are going to be luckier than the others in the short term.

Baccarat players tend to track the win-loss history, as if it made a difference, and then try to guess the outcome of the next hand. As amusing as this might be, the casino staff tries not to laugh and cheerfully supplies pencil and paper for this very purpose.

Randomly choosing between betting on the Player hand or the Banker hand results in a House Percentage that averages about 1.15%. If there is such a thing as the correct way to play Baccarat, it is to always bet on the Banker's Hand and endure the smaller 1.06% House Advantage.

Even though the percentage is relatively low, it is a house game. If you play it much, you will lose. How much you will lose and how fast you will lose it is simply a function of how big your bets are and how many times you bet.

If you want to have the casino comp your room and meals for the day, you would probably have to play Baccarat for a minimum of 4 hours at $100 a hand. Assuming that you play 50 hands an hour, you can expect to lose about $57.50 an hour, or that your room and meals will cost you about $230 a day, on the average.

But, given the ups and downs, it may turn out to be a bigger bite than you intend to take. On the average, you will lose nearly $1,500 something like 58% of the time and win nearly $1,500 about 42% of the time. Of course that's just on the average. You could have a really bad day and lose a whole lot more. Sometimes when it rains, it pours.

Craps

If you enjoy people watching, craps is about as good as it gets. The game just seems to draw characters. The craps tables can be a bit intimidating, but if you find frequent flashes of sound and fury amusing, playing craps can be genuinely amusing. There is seldom a shortage of action.

No casino game is more complicated, in terms of the various options that present themselves during a "roll" or "hand' than Craps. There may be more numbers on the Roulette table, but there are just more things that can be done on the craps table than you can shake a stick at. Every single one of them favors the house.

The game itself is very simple. It's the betting that can be very complicated, if you let it. The more complicated, the better – for the house. If you adhere to two rules: Play Smart and Keep It Simple; on the right craps table you can squeeze the House Percentage down to about 0.18%. If you do the opposite, play dumb and try to get tricky, you can give the house an edge of as much as 16.7%.

First, how to play craps: the shooter tosses the dice against the far end wall of the table. If the dice show a 2 (snake eyes), 3 or 12 (boxcars), it is called craps and everyone who bets on the Pass Line loses. If the first toss is a 7 or 11 (yo-leven), the Pass Line bettors win. If any other number comes up: 4, 5, 6, 8, 9 or 10; it is designated as "the point" and the game continues with the shooter continuing to toss the dice until either the point or a 7 comes up. No other number means anything. Repeating the point number wins the Pass Line bets, with the 7 now a bad number since it loses for the Pass Line bettors and ends the sequence.

Figure 4-2
Right Hand Side of Craps Table Layout

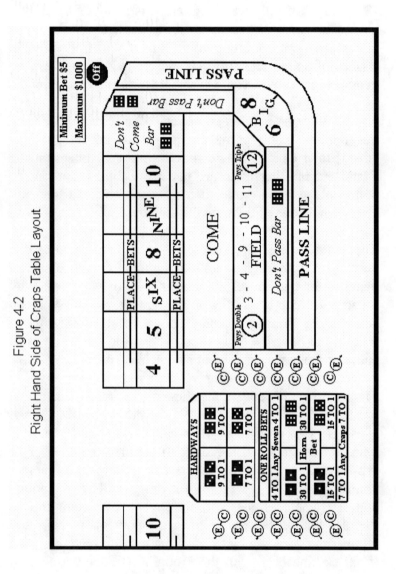

Betting "with" the dice, on the first toss, is called a Pass bet or Pass Line bet. The House Percentage on the Pass Line bet is 1.41%. Not great for the player, but it can be improved on by taking "odds" once a point is established. The dealers place a puck, which is marked 'Off' on one side and "On" on the other, on the appropriately marked number to keep track of the point number.

Craps tables invariably have a placard that states the table minimum, table maximum and the amount of allowable "Odds". In craps, once the shooter has established a point, all those who have a Pass bet in effect are allowed to make another bet at "True Odds" for which there is no House Percentage. Single "Odds" means you can place an "Odds bet" up to the size of your bet on the Pass Line which cuts the House Percentage to 0.85%. Double or 2x Odds means you can place an odds bet up to 2 times the size of your Pass Line bet which cuts the House Percentage to 0.61%. Ten times Odds is about as good as it gets; taking 10 times Odds cuts the House Percentage to 0.18%.

Most casinos allow you to bet a chip or two over single or double Odds so the payout will be "right". For example, if the point is a 6 or 8, True Odds are 6 to 5, which means you should place an Odds bet that is a multiple of 5 units or else the dealer will have to "round down" the payout so you don't get the full benefit. If the point is a 5 or 9, the True Odds are 3 to 2 so the Odds bet should be a multiple of two units. Since the point numbers of 4 and 10 pay 2 for 1, any size Odds bet will work.

The 10 times Odds are always right if you simply put up 10 times the amount on the pass line, since 10 is a multiple of both 2 and 5. It also always works out right if you make Pass bets in multiples of $5 and take full Double Odds.

Depending on the house rule, you may have to adjust your Pass Line bet up a little (you can't subtract from it) to get the Odds bet "right". Ask the dealer if you are in doubt about how much the Odds bet should be. The dealers are supposed to be helpful and usually are.

The "Come" bets work exactly the same way as the Pass Line bets except they are made after the shooter has established a point. It is a separate game, within the game. It just starts when you make the Come bet: a 2, 3 or 12 on the very next toss loses; a 7 or 11 wins; any other number establishes a separate "point" for the Come bet.

If a 4, 5, 6, 8, 9 or 10 comes out, the dealer will pick up the Come bet and move it to the area of the table that is marked to correspond with that number. To take Odds on the Come bet, drop the appropriate amount of chips in the Come area of the table, point to the chips and tell the dealer, for example "Odds on the six". He will then stack the Odds bet, offset slightly, on top of the Come bet.

Just like the pass line point, you want your Come bet number to be repeated before a seven is thrown. You can have several Come bets "working" at the same time as well as a Pass Line bet, depending on how much action you want. The Pass and Come bets must stay on the table until the hand is resolved; until the point or a 7 is thrown. The Odds bets may be removed if the player wishes, at any time. If a 7 shows, they all lose at once.

That's about everything you need to know to get you started and all of the bets you should ever make on the Craps Table.

Ok, the "Don't Pass" and "Don't Come" bets have House Percentages, with Odds, that are marginally better for the player than the House Percentages on the Pass and Come bets, with Odds. But, you need to have a thick hide to bet against the shooter and almost all of the other players at the table. Players who bet against the dice are usually referred to as "wrong way" bettors. If you enjoy that kind of heat, by all means, have at it.

Table 4-2a

Craps Odds	
Type of Wager	House Percentage
Pass Line	1.41%
Don't Pass	1.40%
Come	1.41%
Don't Come	1.40%
Pass/Come with Single Odds	0.85%
Pass/Come with 2x Odds	0.61%
Pass/Come with 10x Odds	0.18%
Don't with Single Odds	0.83%
Don't with 2x Odds	0.59%
Don't with 10x Odds	0.18%

The Don't Pass and Don't Come bets are exactly the opposite of the Pass and Come bets: you are betting that the shooter will lose. Rather than getting odds, you give odds. In order to keep the Percentage on their side, at 1.40%, the house won't pay you if a 12 shows on that first roll; it is a push. Unlike the Pass and come bets, they may be taken down at any time. You can have several Don't Come bets working at a time. If a 7 shows, they all win at once.

None of the other bets on the Craps Table should be made, period. Take the best and leave the rest.

Betting the Pass Line and taking full Odds, while still in the realm of being a house game, gets the House Percentage down into the range that can be offset by generous comps or at least low enough to allow playing Craps to qualify as cheap entertainment. Of course, that depends on how much money you find yourself throwing around.

It is difficult to make apples and apples comparisons between the player's cost of playing Craps and the cost of playing other casino games. For that matter, it is difficult to make comparisons between various betting regimes on the Craps table because of the difference in how many bets get resolved per hour. Ultimately, however, it all comes down to the size of House Percentage, how much you bet and how many times you bet.

Compare the cases where you bet $100 total, 50 times an hour, at House Percentages of 0.18%, 0.61% and 1.41%, as shown on Table 4-3: you lose $9.00, $30.50 and $70.50 per hour, respectively.

It doesn't matter whether you are betting $1 or $100 at a time. The cost is the bite the House Percentage takes out of your play action. The calculation is really simple: multiply the average bet size times number of times you bet, times the House Percentage, divided by 100 (to express the House Percentage as a decimal). On the average, the House takes its Percentage, out of everything wagered. Even though it is obvious when you think about it for even a millisecond, it still helps to see the results in black and white as in Table 4-3.

Table 4-3

Average Loss Rates	
Assume: $100 bets at 50 bets resolved per hour	
House Percentage	Loss Per Hour
0.18%	$9.00
0.61%	$30.50
0.85%	$42.50
1.41%	$70.50
1.52%	$76.00
2.78%	$139.00
4.00%	$200.00
6.67%	$333.50
9.09%	$454.50
11.11%	$555.50
13.89%	$694.50
16.67%	$833.50

With Craps, the variation in the House Percentage, from 0.18% to 16.67%, is nearly 100 fold. Betting Any Seven (Big Red), on the average, will cost you almost 100 times more than making Pass Line bets with 10 times Odds. If you are playing for amusement, how amused can you get? You can be sure that the casino managers and owners find the Any Seven bet hilarious.

Continuing on with the rest of the major bet types in Craps, more or less in increasing order of how much they amuse the House, let's consider the Place bets.

The numbered areas in front of the dealers are there to help you and the dealer keep track of the Place bets. To make a Place bet, which means that you think that a particular number will come up before a 7 does, you drop the amount you wish to wager on the table between you and the dealer and ask him, for example, to "Place the six". The dealer will pick up your chips and position them in the area of the table marked with word "Six", just like he does with the Come bets. Exactly where, in the rectangle, he positions them will correspond to your relative position at the table; so don't move up and down the rail, stay in one place.

You may Place any of the point numbers: 4, 5, 6, 8, 9 or 10. To get the best return on the Place bets, the bets should be in the right multiples. Since the 6 and 8 pay 7 to 6, the bets on them should be multiples of 6, otherwise the payoff is less, rounded down. Similarly, the 5 and 9 pay 7 to 5 and should be bet in multiples of 5. The 4 and 10 pay 9 to 5 and should be bet in multiples of 5. The Place bets may be taken down, removed from the table, at the whim of the player. Unless the player tells the dealer otherwise, the place bets, like the Odds on Come bets, are usually "off" during a "come out" toss.

The Field bet, designated by the large area on the table marked with the words "The Field" and the numbers 2, 3, 4, 9, 10, 11 and 12, is a one roll bet. It gets resolved every time the dice are thrown. Depending on the locality of the game, a 2 is paid double and a 12 is paid triple. At first glance it looks like a good bet since you get so many numbers. However, there are more ways to throw the 5, 6, 7 and 8 than there are for the rest of the numbers. The House Percentage shifts from 2.78% to 5.56% if both the 2 and 12 only pay double.

The Lay bets are another type of Don't bet. You may bet against any of the point numbers by "Laying" the number. The bet works just like the Odds on the Don't Pass or Don't

Come bets. The player pays true odds: 2 to 1 for the 4 or 10, 3 to 2 for the 5 or 9 and 6 to 5 on the 6 and 8; plus a 5% commission for the privilege of making the bet. The 5% commission makes the Lay bets a bit complicated. Since the house must take a minimum of $1, the player should make Lay bets on the 4 and 10 in increments of 40 units, on the 5 and 9 in increments of 30 and on the 6 and 8 in increments of 20 to keep the commission from being rounded up and giving the House more of a Percentage.

Table 4-2b

Craps Odds	
Type of Wager	House Percentage
Place 6 or 8	1.52%
Place 5 or 9	4.00%
Place 4 or 10	6.67%
The Field	2.78%
Lay 4 or 10	2.44%
Lay 5 or 9	3.23%
Lay 6 or 8	4.00%
Buy 4 or 10	4.76%
Buy 5 or 9	4.76%
Buy 6 or 8	4.76%

The Buy bets are "right-way" bets on the point numbers, like the Place bets, but like the Lay bets, they are made at true odds with a 5% commission. Since the Place bets on the 5, 9 and 6, 8 have a lower House Percentage, these numbers should not be "bought". The House Percentage on the 4 and 10 are better for the Buy bets and often you will see bets on the 4 and 10 marked with little buttons marked "Buy". Some casinos only charge the 5% commission on winning Buy bets; others allow the commission to be rounded down. Both reduce the House Percentage, but it still doesn't make Buy bets smart bets.

Table 4-2c

Craps Odds	
Type of Wager	House Percentage
Big 6 or Big 8	9.09%
Hard 6 or 8	9.09%
Hard 4 or 10	11.11%
Eleven	11.11%
Any Craps	11.11%
Three	11.11%
Two	13.89%
Twelve	13.89%
Any Seven	16.67%

Now we get to the Craps bets that are the real turkeys. The Big 6 and Big 8 are prime examples. Essentially they are Place bets that pay 1 to 1 rather than 7 to 6. The casinos offer these bets for people who have absolutely no idea what they are doing. The casinos obviously instruct the dealers not to advise the uninitiated against betting them. It sort of gives you the impression that the casinos would steal flies from a blind spider.

All of the Proposition bets; the "hard ways", Eleven, Craps, Two, Three, Twelve, Any Seven; marked on the felt in front of the "Stickman" are essentially sucker bets. The best that can be said about them is that no one forces you to bet on them. You do it to yourself.

In addition to "Snake Eyes" and "Boxcars", there are a number of names that are used by the "real" craps shooters. The funny part about the Proposition bets is that you can bet them in various combinations that have specific names. "Three-Way-Craps" is a simultaneous wager on the 2, 3 and 12. A "Horn" bet is a simultaneous wager on the 2, 3, 11 and 12. A "Horn High Eleven" is a Horn bet with an extra chip on the 11. A "World" bet is a simultaneous wager on the 2, 3, 7, 11 and 12.

"Hop" bets aren't marked on the table, but the casino will allow you to toss your chips to the top of the Proposition Area and call them; for example: "Hard Eight on the Hop." You might as well toss your money into the trashcan.

The dealers' favorite bets are the "Two-Way" bets. It is a way of tipping the dealers by making a wager for them. A "Two-Way Hard Eight" for example is a combined wager for the player and the dealers. Better is: "Hard Eight for the boys" or even "Dealer hand in", an out and out tip.

You have to give the Craps dealers their due. Craps is not only the most difficult game in the casino to learn, it is the most difficult to deal. Just keeping track of everything is tough. Even the dealers need help from time to time.

That's the raison d'être for the Box man, the only person at the craps table who gets to sit down. Keeping up on everything, making sure the payoffs are right, resolving disputes and guarding the chips is what the Box man is there for. Then, the Box man gets help from the pit boss.

Any kind of wager, that has to do with how the roll of the dice will turn out, will cheerfully be accepted at the Craps table, with the appropriate vigorish, of course. That is part of the charm of the game.

It just seems like there should be some way to bet, amongst the myriad of options, which would give the player an advantage. It is just not so. The variety of schemes designed to "outfox" Craps are legion. They are all crap.

For example, if you try to hedge your Pass line bet with an Any Craps bet, or any of the other Proposition bets, you only wind up giving the house a bigger Percentage. Bet both Pass and Don't Pass to hedge the come out toss and you give the house a bigger Percentage.

Usually the more complicated a hedging scheme is, the bigger is the Percentage it gives to the house. It is like a friend of mine once said: "I feel like a ball-bearing in a can of peas. No matter how you twist it or turn it, I always wind up on the bottom."

One way, a bit cheesy perhaps, to eliminate the House Percentage is to get someone who isn't taking odds to let you play along with him. Take the Odds, tell the dealer you are playing together and ask him to keep the payoff on the Odds separate. The dealers' reactions are amusing. They range from shocked indignation to sly admiration.

Dice games, "throwing the bones", are among the oldest games on record. Over the centuries a considerable body of knowledge has been built up on the various odds and probabilities as well as the various ways to try to beat them. You can be sure that the casinos know them all.

That in no way deters the "would be" Craps millionaires from continuing to re-discover the "secret ways" to beat the house. For just a few hundred dollars you too can become a "Dice Mechanic" and learn how to throw whatever number you wish at your convenience. No matter that the dice are manufactured to be "true cubes" to within one ten thousandth of an inch; No matter that the edges and corners are nearly razor sharp so they will catch in the felt and accentuate the eccentricity of the throw; No matter that the dice have to be thrown against the end of the table that is lined with a rubber-like egg-crate material to angle the bounce in random directions: You too can become a Dice Mechanic and take bushels of money from the casino whenever you wish. Yeah, and pigs can fly.

A visit to the Craps table is like going to the Carnival. It is a microcosm of exuberance, humor, superstition, disaster, greed, stupidity... you name it, and you can find examples at the Craps tables.

The in's and out's of the Craps game are so numerous it would take several books to even touch on the entire story. Improbable characters and ludicrous tales abound. Most of them are true.

Reflect for a moment on the legendary Nick the Greek. His game was Craps. In the history of the game, there has probably been no one who knew more about the game or played it with more intensity. It is said that over his lifetime, he won and lost several fortunes; often with other people's money.

Nick the Greek died broke.

Pai Gow Poker

If you enjoy sitting around a large table and listening to stories about the other player's grandchildren, then Pai Gow Poker is definitely your game. It is the exact opposite of what you find at the Craps tables; it is slow-paced and easy-going. It allows you to contribute to the casino in a more relaxed fashion.

The Pai Gow Poker House Percentage works out to be about 1.5%, provided you don't mess up. If you don't act as the banker as often as possible, every other hand when it is just you and the dealer, then you have messed up big time and the House Percentage goes to about 2.9%, overall.

Unlike Blackjack, Pai Gow Poker is one of those games where the dealer, at the instructions of the casino, will show you the correct way to play. It's called the "House Way" and while it may not be the absolutely perfect way to play every hand, it is close enough for all practical purposes.

The game is pretty straightforward. The dealer shuffles and deals out seven hands of cards from a standard deck 52 card deck to which a Joker has been added. Seven Hands are dealt even though there may be only one player at the table. They are distributed to each of the play spots based on a randomly generated number. The unused hands are discarded. Each of the players arranges the 7 cards into a 5 card High Hand, following standard poker hand rankings, and a Low Hand of 2 cards. The dealer does the same.

Normally the Joker may only be used as an Ace or to fill in a straight or flush. An exception from the standard poker hand rankings is that a low-ball straight of Ace, 2, 3, 4 and 5 is the second highest possible straight.

The rules require that the 5 card hand must always be a little better than the 2 card hand. If you should arrange the 2 hands so that the 2 card hand outranked the 5 card hand, it is an automatic loser. If there is a 5 card flush or a 5 card straight, it is best to put those cards into the 5 card High Hand. The 2 card hand, the Low hand, should be selected to be the second best hand possible. It is usually easier to set up the two hands after you arrange the cards from highest to lowest.

Setting the hands is usually cut and dried. Seldom will you get a hand that offers any real choice in how to arrange the two hands. If you have an Ace, King, 9, 7, 6, 4 and 2, with no flush: You would select the King and 9 to be the 2 card hand. A low hand like this, with no pairs, is a Pai Gow.

Two Pair are usually split up, one pair being put into each hand, with two exceptions: If there is an unpaired ace, it is put into the Low Hand and the two pair are kept together in the High Hand. If both pair are really low, 6's and less, they are also kept together.

All you have to do, should you get confused or want some attention, is to ask the dealer how to arrange the hands. The dealer, and most of the other players, will cheerfully show you how to set your cards.

If both of your hands beat the corresponding dealer hands, you win. If the corresponding dealer hands beat yours, you lose. If one of your hands is better than the corresponding dealer hands and the other is worse, it is a push. Each time you win, you must pay the dealer a 5% commission; 25¢ on a $5 bet, for example.

Generally, about 41.5% of the time it is a push, 30% of the time the dealer wins and 28.5% of the time the player wins. The overall House Percentage is about 2.9%, if the player just bucks the bank. The saving grace is that a player may bank the game as often as every other hand and cut the House Percentage to as low as 1.5% since the House Percentage on the Dealer Hand is 0.1%.

In order to be the Banker, the player must have enough bankroll on the table to payoff the bets of the other players and the dealer who takes a player hand and bets an amount equal to the banking player's last bet. The house dealer will carefully supervise the banking player's hand setting, making sure that it is the House Way, and see to it that all the wagers are resolved correctly. After you have played a few hands, it all becomes very easy and relaxed.

Given that you push 41.5% of the time, there isn't much play action at Pai Gow Poker. Consequently, the casinos don't tend to be very generous with comps for Pai Gow players. At the better casinos, however, the cocktail waitress will come by with free drinks frequently. Consequently, the players tend to be quite convivial.

Should you wish to learn the game, you only need to find a seat at a table that isn't particularly crowded, pull out enough money to cover the table minimum bet and ask the dealer if he or she would help you learn the game. They always seem to be ready to help you learn and will say something like: "I'd be happy to help you. Have a seat. There's nobody here but us chickens."

The casinos do expect that the Pai Gow Poker tables will add to their bottom line. They are seldom wrong.

High Payback Slots

The Slots are a special case. They fit into both the Bad Games category and the Ugly Games category. The House Percentage varies from about 1% to as much as the law allows. Except for the occasional promotional sign that advertises the Percent Payback, you have no way of knowing what the House Percentage might be on a particular machine. Two externally identical machines can, and often do, have wildly different House Percentages.

You can trust the signs that advertise the Percent Payback, at least in Nevada and Atlantic City. The state regulators require that the signs be truthful. They are allowed to be misleading though. Read the small print on the signs. Are they talking about this machine, in particular, the average of a group of machines, or one machine that might be somewhere in this group of machines?

Once you have located a likely suspect, with a low House Percentage, you only need to make sure that you play enough coins on each spin or pull to qualify for the maximum payoff and that you have your Player Club card properly inserted into the card reader. Then, you stuff your money into the machine, push the button or pull the handle and watch the wheels spin and the lights flash.

Sometimes you get some money back and sometimes you don't. Over the long haul the casino will take an amount equal to the House Percentage times your total play action out of your bankroll. You should make sure that you squeeze the maximum amount of comps out of the casino that you can. Otherwise, you are effectively throwing away more of your money than necessary.

Medium Payback Video Poker

Quite a number of Video Poker machines have theoretical Payback Percentages that nearly reach 100%. With a generous Comp policy, the combined return for these little devils can actually exceed 100%. That assumes that the Comp benefits are actually something of real value like cash back or free meals that you would have paid for anyway. Without some incentive, beyond the pleasure of giving some of your money to the casino, as little as that may be for the games discussed here, don't play these games unless the casinos put something in your poke.

If you are going to play Video Poker, you really should play one of the varieties discussed in the previous chapter: Full Pay Joker Poker, 9-5 Deuces Wild, 10-7 Double Bonus or Loose Deuces. Should you be unable to find one of these four, complain bitterly and go hunt one down someplace else. I have known of casino managers who, upon reading a number of comments from the casino's suggestion box about how lousy their Video Poker games were, actually added some Full Pay Video Poker machines.

However, after all else fails, if you find yourself stuck playing one of these second-rate Video Poker games, you should know how to play them well. It just takes a little study to convert a money gobbling ravenous beast into a well-mannered pet that yields up a House Percentage small enough for you to live with.

The two-part Hand Ranking charts shown on Tables 4-4a and b, through Tables 4-11a and b, which are called Strategy Charts or "cheat sheets" are guides to show you how to play to get the best Payback possible from that particular machine. Although they may appear daunting at first, these tables merely show you which of the card combinations, in the initial 5 card hand dealt to you, are the best choices for you to hold with these draw poker games.

For example, suppose you are playing Triple Bonus Poker and you are dealt: 2♠, 6♠, 9♠, Q♠ and Q♦. What should you hold: four to the flush or the pair of queens? Take a look at Table 4-4b, specifically lines 16 and 20. Line 16 ranks a Four card Flush higher than the Low pair 5-Q shown on line 20, so you should hold the four spades and discard the queen of diamonds.

Don't presume that you know which play is best off the top of your head. It all depends on the relative values. Had the pair been kings rather than queens, Line 15 on the first half of the table, Table 4-4a shows that a pair of kings outranks a four card flush. The best play is different for every game.

About all there is to playing like a pro is to follow the advice given by the rank order on the cheat sheet. If you hold the combination that is highest up on the chart, you have made the best choice possible.

Of course you won't remember the correct plays for a particular game until you have played a bunch. Take the book to the casino with you. They don't mind. Or, slap this book down on a copy machine, make a copy of the table you need and take that to the casino.

Also, computer software is available that can teach you how to play any game out there. You can buy Video Poker software from places like the Gambler's Book Shop, gamblersbook.com, at prices ranging from $19.99 to about $150; bargain prices, considering how much you might lose if you don't play correctly. After all, it's your money.

Table 4-4a			
Triple Bonus Poker			
Kings or Better			
5 Coin Pay Table			
Royal Flush	4000		
Straight Flush	250	Flush	35
Four Aces	1200	Straight	20
Four 2s 3s 4s	600	3 of a Kind	15
Four 5s - Ks	375	Two Pair	10
Full House	50	Kings or Better	5
99.8% PayBack			
Always Play Five Coins			
Hold Highest Ranked Combination			

Rank	HandType	EV
1	**5 card Royal Flush**	800.00
2	**4 of a Kind**	98.08
3	**5 card Straight Flush**	50.00
4	**4 card Royal Flush**	19.24
5	**Three Aces**	13.51
6	**Full House**	10.00
7	**Three 2s 3s or 4s**	8.41
8	**5 card Flush**	7.00
9	**Three 5s - Ks**	6.49
10	**5 card Straight**	5.00
11	**4 card Straight Flush**	3.81
12	**4 Card Inside Straight Flush**	2.57
13	**2 Aces**	1.98
14	**Two Pair**	1.77
15	**Two Kings**	1.53

Table 4-4b

	Triple Bonus Poker	
	Always Play 5 Coins	
	Hold Highest Ranked Combination	
Rank	HandType	EV
16	**4 card Flush**	1.38
17	**3 card Royal Flush**	1.34
18	**Two 2s 3s or 4s**	0.94
19	**4 card Straight**	0.85
20	**Low Pair 5s - Qs**	0.81
21	**3 card Straight Flush**	0.68
22	**3 card Low Inside Straight Flush**	0.57
23	**3 card Inside Str Flush King High**	0.56
24	**4 card Ace High Straight**	0.55
25	**3 card Flush - Ace + King High**	0.55
26	**2 card Ace - King Royal**	0.55
27	**3 card inside Str Flush - 2 gaps**	0.46
28	**3 card Flush - 1 High Card**	0.45
29	**2 card King High Royal**	0.43
30	**1 Ace**	0.43
31	**4 card Inside Straight**	0.43
32	**2 High Cards Ace + King**	0.42
33	**1 King**	0.39
34	**2 card Jack - 10 Royal**	0.35
35	**3 card Flush**	0.35
36	**2 card Q High Royal**	0.33
37	**2 card Straight Flush**	0.30
38	**3 card Straight**	0.28
39	**2 card Straight Flush - 1 gap**	0.28
40	**Nothing - Draw Five**	0.26

Table 4-5a

Jacks or Better 9-6
5 Coin Pay Table

Royal Flush	4000
Straight Flush	250
4 of a Kind	125
Full House (9 for 1)	45
Flush (6 for 1)	30
Straight	20
3 of a Kind	15
Two Pair	10
Jacks or Better	5

99.5% PayBack
Always Play Five Coins
Hold Highest Ranked Combination

Rank	HandType	EV
1	**5 card Royal Flush**	800.00
2	**5 card Straight Flush**	50.00
3	**4 of a Kind**	25.00
4	**4 card Royal Flush**	18.49
5	**5 card Full House**	9.00
6	**5 card Flush**	6.00
7	**3 of a Kind**	4.30
8	**5 card Straight**	4.00
9	**4 card Straight Flush**	3.53
10	**Two Pair**	2.60
11	**4 card Inside Straight Flush**	2.34

Table 4-5b

Rank	HandType	EV
Jacks or Better 9-6 *Always Play Five Coins* *Hold Highest Ranked Combination*		
12	High Pair	1.54
13	3 card Royal Flush	1.53
14	4 card Flush	1.21
15	4 card King High Straight	0.87
16	Low Pair	0.82
17	4 card Queen High Straight	0.81
18	4 card Jack High Straight	0.74
19	3 card Jack High Straight Flush	0.73
20	4 card Low Straight	0.68
21	3 card Inside Str Flush 1 Hi Card	0.64
22	3 card Straight Flush	0.63
23	2 card Queen - Jack Royal	0.62
24	4 card Ace High Inside Straight	0.60
25	2 High card Royal Flush	0.59
26	3 card Low Inside Straight Flush	0.54
27	3 cards King Queen Jack	0.52
28	2 card Jack - 10 Royal	0.50
29	2 High Cards	0.49
30	2 card King or Queen - 10 Royal	0.49
31	1 High Card	0.47
32	3 card Inside Str Flush - 2 gaps	0.43
33	Nothing - Draw Five	0.36

Table 4-6a				
Double Deuces				
5 Coin Pay Table				
Royal Flush	4000	4 of a Kind		20
Four Deuces	2000	Full House		15
Wild Royal	125	Flush		10
5 of a Kind	80	Straight		10
Straight Flush	55	3 of a Kind		5
99.6% PayBack				

Rank	HandType	EV
	With no Deuces	
1	**5 card Royal Flush**	800.00
2	**4 card Royal Flush**	19.57
3	**5 card Straight Flush**	11.00
4	**4 of a Kind**	5.02
5	**5 card Full House**	3.00
6	**5 card Flush**	2.00
7	**5 card Straight**	2.00
8	**4 card Straight Flush**	1.91
9	**3 of a Kind**	1.83
10	**4 card Inside Straight Flush**	1.60
11	**3 card Royal Flush**	1.39
12	**1 Pair (never 2 Pair)**	0.52
13	**3 card Straight Flush**	0.53
14	**4 card Flush**	0.51
15	**4 card Straight**	0.51
16	**3 card Straight Flush 1 gap**	0.47
17	**3 card Straight Flush 2 gap**	0.38
18	**2 card Jack - 10 Royal**	0.38
19	**2 card Queen High Royal**	0.35
20	**2 card King High Royal**	0.33
21	**4 card Inside Straight**	0.34
22	**Nothing - Draw five**	0.33

Table 4-6b

Rank	HandType	EV
Double Deuces *Always Hold Every Deuce* *Hold Highest Ranked Combination*		
	With 3 Deuces	
1	5 card Wild Royal	25.00
2	3 Deuces	23.00
	With 2 Deuces	
1	5 card Wild Royal	25.00
2	5 of a Kind	16.00
3	5 card Straight Flush	11.00
4	4 of a Kind	5.02
5	4 card Wild Royal	4.79
6	2 Deuces	3.60
	With 1 Deuce	
1	5 card Wild Royal	25.00
2	5 of a Kind	16.00
3	5 card Straight Flush	11.00
4	4 of a Kind	5.02
5	4 card Wild Royal	3.70
6	5 card Full House	3.00
7	4 card Straight Flush	2.55
8	4 Card Straight Flush with 1 gap	2.23
9	5 card Flush	2.00
10	5 card Straight	2.00
11	4 Card Straight Flush with 2 gap	1.91
12	3 of a Kind	1.83
13	3 card Wild Royal	1.23
14	3 card Str Flush (7 High & Higher)	1.15
15	3 card Inside Straight Flush 1 gap	1.04
16	1 Deuce	1.03

Table 4-7a

Bonus Poker
5 Coin Pay Table
Royal Flush 4000 Coins

Straight Flush	250	Flush	25
Four Aces	400	Straight	20
Four 2s 3s 4s	200	3 of a Kind	15
Four 5s - Ks	125	Two Pair	10
Full House	40	Jacks or Better	5

99.2% PayBack
Always Play Five Coins
Hold Highest Ranked Combination

Rank	Handtype	EV
1	**5 card Royal Flush**	800.00
2	**5 card Straight Flush**	50.00
3	**4 of a Kind**	32.69
4	**4 card Royal Flush**	18.38
5	**5 card Full House**	8.00
6	**5 card Flush**	5.00
7	**3 of a Kind**	4.58
8	**5 card Straight**	4.00
9	**4 card Straight Flush**	3.40
10	**Two Pair**	2.51
11	**4 card Inside Straight Flush**	2.17
12	**3 Card Royal Flush**	1.72
13	**High Pair**	1.61

Table 4-7b

Rank	Handtype	EV
	Bonus Poker	
	Always Play Five Coins	
	Hold Highest Ranked Combination	
Rank	**Handtype**	**EV**
14	**4 Card Flush**	1.02
15	**4 card King High Straight**	0.87
16	**Low Pair**	0.81
17	**4 card Q or J High Straight**	0.81
18	**3 card Q J 9 Straight Flush**	0.70
19	**3 card J High Straight Flush**	0.70
20	**4 card Low Straight**	0.68
21	**2 card Q - J Royal**	0.61
22	**3 card Inside Str Flush - 1 HC**	0.60
23	**3 card Straight Flush**	0.60
24	**4 card Ace High Straight**	0.60
25	**2 High Card Royal**	0.59
26	**4 card Ace High Inside Straight**	0.53
27	**3 cards King Queen Jack**	0.52
28	**3 card Low Inside Straight Flush**	0.50
29	**2 card J - 10 Royal**	0.49
30	**2 High Cards**	0.49
31	**2 card Q - 10 Royal**	0.48
32	**1 High Card**	0.46
33	**3 card inside Str Flush - 2 gaps**	0.40
34	**Nothing - Draw Five**	0.36

Table 4-8a

	Deuces Joker Wild 1000 Jackpot				

5 Coin Pay Table

5 Wild Cards	10000	Straight Flush	30
Royal Flush	4000	4 of a Kind	15
4 Deuces	125	Full House/Flus	15
Wild Royal Flusl	60	Straight	10
5 of a Kind	45	3 of a Kind	5

99.1% PayBack
Always Play Five Coins
Hold Highest Ranked Combination

Rank	HandType	EV
	With no Wild Cards	
1	**5 card Royal Flush**	800.00
2	**4 card Royal Flush**	18.48
3	**5 card Straight Flush**	6.00
4	**4 of a Kind**	3.63
5	**5 card Full House**	3.00
6	**5 card Flush**	3.00
7	**5 card Straight**	2.00
8	**3 of a Kind**	1.66
9	**4 card Straight Flush**	1.50
10	**3 card Q J 10 Royal**	1.37
11	**4 card Inside Str Flush**	1.31
12	**3 card Royal**	1.26
13	**4 card Flush**	0.81
14	**3 card Straight Flush**	0.56
15	**2 Pair**	0.56
16	**1 Pair**	0.55
17	**4 card Straight**	0.54
18	**3 card Str Flush 1 gap**	0.49
19	**3 card Str Flush 2 gap**	0.43
20	**2 card Q/J/10 Royal**	0.38
21	**4 card Inside Straight**	0.37
22	**Nothing - Draw five**	0.36

Table 4-8b

Rank	HandType	EV	
	With 4 Wild Cards		
1	4 Wild Cards only	66.15	
	With 3 Wild Cards		
1	5 card Wild Royal	12.00	
2	5 of a Kind (10 - A)	9.00	
3	3 Wild Cards	6.93	
	With 2 Wild Cards		
1	5 card Wild Royal	12.00	
2	5 of a Kind	9.00	
3	5 card Straight Flush	6.00	
4	4 of a Kind	3.63	
5	4 card Wild Royal	3.33	
6	4 card Straight Flush	2.71	
7	4 card Inside SF 2 gaps	2.46	
8	2 Wild Cards	2.35	
	With 1 Wild Card		
1	5 card Wild Royal	12.00	
2	5 of a Kind	9.00	
3	5 card Straight Flush	6.00	
4	4 of a Kind	5.85	
5	5 card Full House	3.00	
6	5 card Flush	3.00	
7	4 card Wild Royal	2.75	
8	5 card Straight	2.00	
9	4 card Straight Flush	2.00	
10	4 Card SF w/ 1gap	1.81	
11	3 of a Kind	1.66	
12	4 Card SF w/2gap	1.63	
13	3 card Wild Royal	1.21	
14	3 card Str Flush	1.08	
15	4 card Flush	1.00	
16	3 card Inside SF 2 gaps	0.99	
17	1 Wild Card	0.97	

Deuces Joker Wild 1000 Jackpot

Table 4-9a

Bonus Deluxe			
5 Coin Pay Table			
Royal Flush	4000	Flush	30
Straight Flush	250	Straight	20
4 of a Kind	400	3 of a Kind	15
Full House	40	Two Pair /JorB	5
98.5% PayBack			
Always Play Five Coins			
Hold Highest Ranked Combination			

Rank	Handtype	EV
1	5 card Royal Flush	800.00
2	4 of a Kind	80.00
3	5 card Straight Flush	50.00
4	4 card Royal Flush	18.88
5	5 card Full House	8.00
6	3 of a Kind	6.58
7	5 card Flush	6.00
8	5 card Straight	4.00
9	4 card Straight Flush	3.53
11	4 card Inside Straight Flush	2.34
10	Two Pair	1.56
12	High Pair	1.52
13	3 card Royal Flush	1.51

Table 4-9b

Bonus Deluxe		
Rank	Handtype	EV
14	4 card Flush	1.28
15	4 card K High Straight	0.87
16	Low Pair	0.81
17	4 card Q High Straight	0.81
18	4 card J High Straight	0.74
19	3 card J High Straight Flush	0.70
20	4 card Low Straight	0.68
21	3 card Inside Str Flush 1 or 2 HC	0.61
22	3 card Straight Flush	0.61
23	4 card Ace High Straight	0.60
24	2 High card Royal Flush	0.56
25	3 card Low Inside Str Flush	0.51
26	3 cards King-Queen-Jack	0.49
27	2 card Jack - 10 Royal	0.48
28	2 High Cards	0.47
29	2 card Queen - 10 Royal	0.46
30	1 High Card	0.44
31	3 card inside Str Flush - 2 gaps	0.42
32	4 card Inside Straight	0.34
33	Nothing - Draw Five	0.32

Table 4-10a

Jacks or Better 8-5 Progressive			
5 Coin Pay Table			
Royal Flush - Progressive Amount			
Straight Flush	250	Straight	20
4 of a Kind	125	3 of a Kind	15
Full House	40	Two Pair	10
Flush	25	Jacks or Better	5
97.2% PayBack at 4000 Coins			
97.9% - 5200 Coins			
100% - 8700 Coins			
Always Play Five Coins			
Hold Highest Ranked Combination			

Rank	Handtype	EV
1	**5 card Royal Flush**	>800.00
2	**5 card Straight Flush**	50.00
3	**4 of a Kind**	25.00
4	**4 card Royal Flush**	23.49
5	**5 card Full House**	8.00
6	**5 card Flush**	5.00
7	**3 of a Kind**	4.24
8	**5 card Straight**	4.00
9	**4 card Straight Flush**	3.38
10	**Two Pair**	2.51
11	**4 card Inside Straight Flush**	2.17
12	**3 card Royal Flush**	1.72
13	**High Pair**	1.54

games. The 8-5 designation refers to the payoff for a
Straight Flush at $40 and the Fourof a Kind at $125.
This strat chart is somewhat revised for simplicity. Be sure
to check off at the payoffs on the pay table against the chart
shown in table 4-10a. The pay line is identical to that in
the Deuces at Better pay table.

Table 11-x

Deuces Wild Video Poker Pay Table
100.78% Payback

Table 4-10b

Rank	Handtype	EV
	Jacks or Better 8-5 Progressive	
	Always Play Five Coins *Hold Highest Ranked Combination*	
14	4 card Flush	1.02
15	4 card King High Straight	0.87
16	Low Pair	0.81
17	4 card Q or J High Straight	0.77
18	3 card Jack High Straight Flush	0.70
19	4 card Low Straight	0.68
20	3 card Inside Str Flush 1 or 2 HC	0.60
21	3 card Straight Flush	0.60
22	2 card Queen - Jack Royal	0.60
23	4 card Ace High Straight	0.60
24	2 High Card Royal	0.57
25	4 card Ace High Inside Straight	0.53
26	3 cards King Queen Jack	0.52
27	2 card Jack - 10 Royal	0.50
28	2 High Cards	0.49
29	2 card High Card -10 Royal	0.48
30	3 card Low Inside Straight Flush	0.48
31	1 High Card	0.47
32	3 card inside Str Flush - 2 gaps	0.40
33	Nothing - Draw Five	0.36

Table 4-11a

Double Double Bonus				
5 Coin Pay Table				
Royal Flush	4000	Four 5s - Ks	250
Straight Flush	250	Full House	45
Four Aces	800	Flush	25
with 2 3 or 4	2000	Straight	20
Four 2s 3s 4s	400	3 of a Kind	15
with A 2 3 or 4	800	Two Pair /J or B	5
97.8% PayBack				

Rank	Handtype	EV
1	5 card Royal Flush	800.00
2	4 of a Kind	77.74
3	5 card Straight Flush	50.00
4	4 card Royal Flush	18.95
5	3 Aces	12.40
6	5 card Full House	9.00
7	3 of a Kind	6.33
8	5 card Flush	5.00
9	5 card Straight	4.00
10	4 card Straight Flush	3.43
11	4 card Inside Straight Flush	2.17
12	Pair Aces	1.91
13	Two Pair	1.68
14	High Pair	1.45
15	3 card Royal Flush	1.41

Table 4-11b

Rank	Handtype	EV
	Double Double Bonus	
	Always Play Five Coins	
	Hold Highest Ranked Combination	
16	4 card Flush	1.02
17	4 card King High Straight	0.87
18	Pair of 2s 3s 4s	0.87
19	4 card Q or J High Straight	0.77
20	Pair 5s - 10s	0.73
21	4 card low Straight	0.68
22	3 card J High Straight Flush	0.65
23	4 card Ace High Straight	0.60
24	3 card Inside Str Flush 1 or 2 HC	0.57
25	2 High card Royal Flush	0.56
26	3 card Straight Flush	0.54
27	3 cards King-Queen-Jack	0.49
28	2 card Jack - 10 Royal	0.46
29	1 Ace	0.46
30	2 High Cards	0.45
31	3 card Low Inside Str Flush	0.44
32	2 card King or Queen - 10 Royal	0.44
33	1 High Card	0.43
34	3 card Inside Str Flush 2-gaps	0.36
35	4 card Inside Straight	0.34
36	Nothing - Draw Five	0.33

Triple Bonus Video Poker

The hand ranking charts, cheat sheets, for Triple Bonus
Video Poker are shown on Table 4-4a and Table 4-4b. In
addition to the 5 coin Pay Table shown on Table 4-4a, the
complete Pay Table is shown on Table 4-4c to help you
identify this game unambiguously. Unless this Pay Table
exactly matches the one on the machine that you are considering playing, the cheat sheets do not apply and the theoretical Paybacks are different.

Table 4-4c

Triple Bonus Video Poker Pay Table 99.8% Payback					
	1 Coin	2 Coins	3 Coins	4 Coins	5 Coins
Royal Flush	250	500	750	1000	4000
Straight Flush	50	100	150	200	250
Four Aces	240	480	720	960	1200
Four 2s 3s 4s	120	240	360	480	600
Four 5s - Ks	75	150	225	300	375
Full House	10	20	30	40	50
Flush	7	14	21	28	35
Straight	4	8	12	16	20
3 of a Kind	3	6	9	12	15
Two Pair	2	4	6	8	10
Kings or Better	1	2	3	4	5

The interest in this variety of Video Poker stems from the
very high payouts for the various denominations of Four of
a Kind, particular that for 4 Aces. It makes it really fun
when you are hitting them, but the game is a killer when
you're not. The cost is that it is a Kings or Better game. A
pair of queens or jacks pays nothing, which more than
offsets the higher bonus payouts.

The best play tactics are rather complicated for this game, with some unusual features. A number of the play choices are not even remotely intuitive.

For example, as you can see on Table 4-4b, line 26, an ace-king 2 card Royal is not as good a hold as a 3 card flush with 2 high cards, shown on line 25; that is, the same two card Royal with a matched suit small card. Although the Expected Values (EV) are the same to two decimal places, it is marginally better to hold for the plain flush rather than the Royal flush.

With Triple Bonus poker, a two card straight flush is a worth holding and so is a two card inside straight flush. So is a three card straight, but not a three card inside straight.

As you might expect, with the high bonus value for Aces, you should take every opportunity to make 4 Aces. A full house containing three Aces should be broken up so you can hit the 4 Aces. If you get two pair containing a pair of Aces, you should discard the small pair. These plays are indicated on the cheat sheets by three Aces ranking higher than a full house and two Aces outranking two pair.

The lack of a payoff for pairs of queens and jacks can be rather distracting and annoying until you get used to it. It is easy to forget that they are just low pairs. After playing so many varieties of Jacks or Better poker, playing Kings or Better just doesn't seem natural.

The theoretical Payback for this game is 99.8%, making it quite playable, in the light of even a little comp value from the casino. In the absence of one of the other Video Poker games that has a higher return, Triple Bonus Video Poker is not a bad choice. Just keep your cheat sheets close by.

9-6 Jacks or Better Video Poker

Jacks or Better games are pretty much the standard Video Poker games. Unfortunately the lower paying varieties tend to dominate the floor space in most casinos. The designation 9-6 for the Full Pay variety of Jacks or Better stems from the payoff values for full house and flush as shown on Table 4-5c.

Table 4-5c

(9-6) Jacks or Better Video Poker Pay Table 99.5% Payback					
	1 Coin	2 Coins	3 Coins	4 Coins	5 Coins
Royal Flush	250	500	750	1000	4000
Straight Flush	50	100	150	200	250
4 of a Kind	25	50	75	100	125
Full House	9	18	27	36	45
Flush	6	12	18	24	30
Straight	4	8	12	16	20
3 of a Kind	3	6	9	12	15
Two Pair	2	4	6	8	10
Jacks or Better	1	2	3	4	5

If the Pay Table shows only an 8-5 payoff for the full house and flush, respectively, the Payback drops to 97.2%. With a 7-5 machine, the Payback is 96.1% and with the 6-5 variety (not a pretty sight) the Payback is a paltry 95%. Even worse are the machines that cheat on the two pair Payback. You simply should not play the lower paying varieties of Jacks or Better. Stick with the 9-6 variety (or better, if you can find them), or don't play them at all.

The reason for avoiding the lower paying games is quite simple: money. It makes a big difference in your loss rate, both your bankroll and enjoyment will take a beating.

Since more than 500 hands are usually played per hour, on a 25¢ machine with 5 coins played per hand, the play action is $625 per hour. Your loss rate with the so-called Full Pay, 9-6 variety, will average $3.13 per hour. With the 8-5 it will average $17.50 per hour. With the 7-5, it is $24.38 and with the 6-5 it is a healthy $31.25 an hour. Multiply by 4 for the $1 machines.

Those little differences on the Pay Table can make a significant difference in how much you contribute to the casino. If you wish to pay $31.25 per hour rather than $3.13 per hour for your entertainment, you will certainly gladden the hearts of the casino owners.

Personally, I find the higher paying machines to be a lot more entertaining than the lower paying machines. Being rapidly plucked doesn't amuse me much. Besides, the casinos usually will give you about the same comp value regardless of which machine you play.

In some casinos, like at the Stratosphere Casino in Las Vegas, you will occasionally run across a 10-6 or a 9-7 Jacks or Better Video Poker machine. These will Payback more than 100% if you play them correctly. You can actually make a little money, $4 to $5 per hour on the 25¢ machines, and the casino will reward you for playing. The cheat sheets for the standard 9-6 game, shown on Table 6-5a and Table 6-5b can be used with little or no modification to play them.

There is no difference at all between the correct play for the 10-6 Jacks or Better from the play shown on Tables 4-5a and 4-5b for the 9-6 variety. With the 9-7 variety, the hand rankings need to be modified only by the promotion of a 3 card Inside Straight Flush with 2 gaps, on line 32, up in ranking ahead of 1 High Card, on line 31, as well as the addition of the 2 card A-10 Royals to the bottom of the hand ranking chart.

If you play Video Poker at all, the Jacks or Better games are the ones you will encounter most often. The 9-6 Jacks or Better is certainly the standard variety and you should take the time to learn how to play it correctly.

Keep a copy of Table 4-5, the hand ranking chart, on your person at all times when you play this game. Even after you feel that you have it down cold, it is best to have a hard copy to refer to when you occasionally blank out.

Fundamental tactical rules include:
Never hold a kicker.
Never draw to an inside straight.
With 3 unsuited high cards, do not hold an ace.

Note that two pair, line 10 on Table 4-5a, outranks a pair of high cards, line 12 on the second half -Table 4-5b. Since there are no bonuses for Four of a Kind and the full house payoff is a healthy 9 for 1, you should never break up two pair; other games, other tactics, but not here.

Although the hand ranking chart indicates that two high cards outrank a 2 card Q-10 Royal (on lines 29 and 30), an exception to this rule is: if a hand contains an unsuited Ace with a Queen and Ten which are suited, it is better to hold the Q-10 combination.

Although the theoretical Payback with best play is 99.54%, if you can find one of the games with a better Payback, you should play the higher Payback Percentage game.

Double Deuces Video Poker

Double Deuces is a fun game, if you hit Four Deuces. The payoff is, as the name implies, double that of the regular Deuces Wild game and half that of the Royal Flush payoff.

On the average you should hit the Four Deuces about once in every 10 hours of play, almost 10 times more frequently than you will hit the Royal Flush. The Pay Table on Table 4-6c, shows that the payoff for the 4 of a Kind is reduced from 5 for 1 to 4 for 1, to compensate the casino for the more generous Four Deuces pay.

Table 4-6c

Double Deuces Video Poker Pay Table 99.6% Payback					
	1 Coin	2 Coins	3 Coins	4 Coins	5 Coins
Royal Flush	250	500	750	1000	4000
Four Deuces	400	800	1200	1600	2000
Wild Royal	25	50	75	100	125
5 of a Kind	16	32	48	64	80
Straight Flush	11	22	33	44	55
4 of a Kind	4	8	12	16	20
Full House	3	6	9	12	15
Flush	2	4	6	8	10
Straight	2	4	6	8	10
3 of a Kind	1	2	3	4	5

The 4 of a Kind payoff on the Full Pay, 9-5 Deuces Wild accounts for a little over 32% of the total Payback. Cutting that back by one fifth, 6.4%, and then increasing the payoff for the 4 Deuces, 5 of a Kind and Straight Flush doesn't quite favor the player. Now who is surprised by that?

Be careful that you don't find yourself playing a Double Deuces variety that is a close approximation to the one shown here but doesn't quite have the right Pay Table. Imposters abound. They seldom have better Pay Tables.

Again, if you can find a Full Pay Deuces Wild game, you should play that and not this. If both varieties are available, playing this game will tend to confuse your play on the regular Deuces Wild.

However if this is the best you can come up with, learn to play the game right. Focus right in on the cheat sheet shown on Tables 4-6a and 4-6b, make a copy and keep it handy at all times.

On Table 4-6b, the section that is applicable to hands that contain three deuces shows that you should only hold a Wild Royal or Three Deuces. You shouldn't keep Five of a Kind when the hand contains Three Deuces. The bonus value of Four Deuces makes it more profitable to hold only Three Deuces and discard any other pair that would make Five of a Kind.

Similarly for hands containing Two Deuces, the bonus value modifies the normal Deuces Wild play: a Straight Flush should not be held. It is best to simply hold only the Two Deuces.

Although the value of partial Straight Flushes is increased with the Double Deuces variety over those with the Full Pay, 9-5 Deuces Wild, it makes little difference in the way those hands are played.

The 99.6% Payback makes this version of Double Deuces Video Poker playable, if the casino gives good comps. Otherwise, find something else to play or play somewhere else that offers higher paying games.

Bonus Poker Video Poker

Bonus Poker is simply a Jacks or Better game that pays more for Four Aces and Four 2's, 3's and 4's than regular Jacks or Better. The 8-5 payoff (8 for 1 for a Full House and 5 for 1 for a Flush) compared to the 9-6 payoff with the Full Pay game winds up cutting the Payback Percentage from 99.5% to 99.2% as shown on Table 4-7c.

Table 4-7c

Bonus Poker Video Poker Pay Table 99.2% Payback					
	1 Coin	2 Coins	3 Coins	4 Coins	5 Coins
Royal Flush	250	500	750	1000	4000
Straight Flush	50	100	150	200	250
Four Aces	80	160	240	320	400
Four 2s 3s 4s	40	80	120	160	200
Four 5s - Ks	25	50	75	100	125
Full House	8	16	24	32	40
Flush	5	10	15	20	25
Straight	4	8	12	16	20
3 of a Kind	3	6	9	12	15
Two Pair	2	4	6	8	10
Jacks or Better	1	2	3	4	5

The bonus payoffs serve the purpose of increasing the excitement value. Hitting Four Aces on a 25¢ machine pays off $100. But, it is not worth it. You really should stick to playing something with a higher Theoretical Payback. But then, there are a lot worse machines out there and if this is the best you can come up, be prepared to pay about $5 an hour, on the average, for the pleasure.

You should understand that $5 an hour, on the average, doesn't mean that your fortune might not go up and down by as much as two or three thousand dollars, on a 25¢ machine. It will. What it means is that over many millions of hands; that is, for you and all the people it takes to grind out many millions of hands; the collective group will contribute about $5 an hour to the casino, on the average.

Being a Jacks or Better Video Poker game, as you might expect, the best way to play the Bonus Poker game, as shown on Tables 4-7a and 4-7b, is very similar to the Full Pay, 9-6 Jacks or Better. Compare the cheat sheets.

Like the regular Jacks or Better fundamental rules include:
Never hold a kicker.
Never draw to an inside straight.
With 3 unsuited high cards, do not hold the ace.

Although it is tempting to make special accommodation in the play tactics for hands such as a full house containing three Aces, the mathematics do not justify discarding the low pair. Trust the numbers. The casinos do.

Since the entire family of Jacks or Better games have basically the same best play tactics with a few distinctive differences, perhaps the best way to learn the differences in play tactics is to invest in one of the computer software packages that are available for learning and analyzing Video Poker games. They are available from places like the Gambler's Book Shop (gamblersbook.com) for as little as $19.99 and are well worth the price.

With a theoretical Payback of 99.2%, Bonus Poker is quite playable, provided you play correctly and the casino has a decent comp policy to make up for some of your outlay. Again, if you have a higher paying choice, one with a higher Payback Percentage, go for that and not for this.

Deuces and Joker Wild Video Poker

There are several varieties of Deuces and Joker Wild Video Poker. The pick of the litter is the 10,000 Jackpot variety, as illustrated by the Pay Table shown on Table 4-8c.

Table 4-8c

Deuces & Joker Wild (10,000) Video Poker Pay Table 99.1% Payback					
	1 Coin	2 Coins	3 Coins	4 Coins	5 Coins
5 Wild Cards	400	800	1200	1600	10000
Royal Flush	250	500	750	1000	4000
4 Deuces	25	50	75	100	125
Wild Royal Flush	12	24	36	48	60
5 of a Kind	9	18	27	36	45
Straight Flush	6	12	18	24	30
4 of a Kind	3	6	9	12	15
Full House/Flush	3	6	9	12	15
Straight	2	4	6	8	10
3 of a Kind	1	2	3	4	5

Don't be surprised if you can't find this game anywhere. Although it was quite common in the early 1990's, it is rare today. I had thought it was entirely extinct until I just happened to run across several machines in three different casinos. Sometimes they come back into vogue.

Of course, the attraction for this game is the huge payoff for hitting the Five Wild Cards. Unfortunately, it is nearly as improbable as hitting the lottery. I have only known of one instance of anyone actually hitting the big one on this machine. So, it does happen, but don't get your hopes up too high if you happen across one of these dinosaurs.

The high bonus payoff, in effect, reduces the payoff for the smaller hands, and unless you actually play this game long enough to hit the Five Wild payoff, you will be playing at a considerable disadvantage. If you take the Five Wild pay-off out of action, the game pays considerably less than the listed 99.1%

The cheat sheet on Tables 4-8a and 4-8b illustrates the best play tactics for this game. Note that like the other wild card games, the best play tactics are divided into sections that correspond to how many wild cards you are initially dealt. Although it makes the cheat sheet look complicated, it is actually quite easy to find the correct play since the sections are each relatively small.

It is essentially a different game for hands with different numbers of wild cards. More is better and simpler. For example, with four wild cards in the initial hand, you simply throw away the stranger and go for Five Wild.

With 3 Wild cards, the only hands you should hold are a Wild Royal Flush or the Five of a Kinds, Tens through Aces. These should be held because the two high cards re-duce the possibility of drawing a Wild Royal. With the low Five of a Kinds, you should just hold the wild cards.

The Value of the partial Straight Flushes is relatively high and, therefore, should be held more frequently than with other wild card games, such as 9-5 Deuces Wild.

With expert play, the theoretical Payback Percentage for this variety of Deuces and Joker Wild Video Poker is 99.1%, but it feels a lot worse over the short term. Unless you can't find anything better and the casino is really gen-erous with its comps, you probably shouldn't even consider playing this antique.

Bonus Deluxe Video Poker

Bonus Deluxe Video Poker is a Jacks or Better game, very similar to the Full Pay Jacks or Better game, that pays extra for any Four of a Kind and shorts the payoff on Two Pair. As shown on Table 4-9c, the payoff for Four of a Kind is 80 for 1 rather than 25 for 1. The Two Pair payoff is reduced to 1 for 1, which more than offsets the bonus value for the Four of a Kind. This game is marginal at best.

Table 4-9c

Bonus Deluxe Video Poker Pay Table 98.5% Payback					
	1 Coin	2 Coins	3 Coins	4 Coins	5 Coins
Royal Flush	250	500	750	1000	4000
Straight Flush	50	100	150	200	250
4 of a Kind	80	160	240	320	400
Full House	8	16	24	32	40
Flush	6	12	18	24	30
Straight	4	8	12	16	20
3 of a Kind	3	6	9	12	15
Two Pair	1	2	3	4	5
Jacks or Better	1	2	3	4	5

It is similar to the Full Pay, 9-6 Jacks or Better game in terms of the best play tactics. There are, however, some tactical differences that reduce the Payback Percentage if the appropriate play adjustments are not made. Although minor differences seem trivial, taking advantage of them can make a significant difference in the House Percentage.

One of the main differences between Bonus Deluxe and its Full Pay cousin is that the value of Three of a Kind is greatly increased due to the higher payoff value for Four of a Kind. It outranks a 5 card Flush. However, it is only an apparent difference, not a tactical difference since a hand cannot contain both combinations at the same time.

A real tactical difference is that a Four Card Ace High Straight (Table 4-9b, line 23) outranks all Two High Card Royal Flushes (Table 4-9b line 24). It even outranks the fairly strong Queen Jack combination.

Also, unlike the Full Pay, 9-6 Jacks or Better game, it is better, with Bonus Deluxe, to hold a four card inside straight than to draw five cards.

Like the regular Jacks or Better fundamental rules include:
Never hold a kicker.
Never draw to an inside straight.
With 3 unsuited high cards, do not hold the ace.

As with 9-6 Jacks or Better, a Jack and Ten two card Royal Flush outranks all two unsuited high card combinations, except for the Jack and Queen combination.

With the theoretical Payback Percentage only at 98.5% with best play, Bonus Deluxe is certainly not the best choice you can make. The fact that there are Video Poker games that are a lot worse hardly justifies playing this one. Only when and if these games are the subject of casino promotions, such as tournaments, are they worth the time and trouble it takes to learn their idiosyncrasies.

Unless the casino is offering some special inducement to play this particular game, or it is the instrument in a tournament of some sort, you should look around. Find something else. With a little effort you should be able to locate a Video Poker game that offers a better Payback Percentage than this one.

8-5 Jacks or Better Video Poker, Progressive Jackpot

The Jacks or Better Video Poker games that have a progressive jackpot; that is, a jackpot on a particular machine or bank of machines that just keeps growing until someone hits it, are usually the 8-5 variety of Jacks or Better, with a Pay Table like that shown on Table 4-10c. Without a progressive jackpot, playing the 8-5 variety of Jacks or Better is virtually impossible to justify.

Table 4-10c

(8-5) Jacks or Better Progressive Video Poker Pay Table 97.2% Payback at 4000 Coins 97.9% Payback at 5200 Coins 100% Payback at 8700 Coins					
	1 Coin	2 Coins	3 Coins	4 Coins	5 Coins
Royal Flush	250	500	750	1000	Prog.
Straight Flush	50	100	150	200	250
4 of a Kind	25	50	75	100	125
Full House	8	16	24	32	40
Flush	5	10	15	20	25
Straight	4	8	12	16	20
3 of a Kind	3	6	9	12	15
Two Pair	2	4	6	8	10
Jacks or Better	1	2	3	4	5

With only a 4,000 coin jackpot for the Royal Flush, there is virtually no justification for playing this game with its House Percentage near 3%.

As the progressive jackpot climbs, the game becomes more attractive, but even with the jackpot over 5,200 coins, the game is sill marginal with a strong 2% House Edge. Seldom will you find a Jacks or Better game that has a progressive jackpot as high as 5,200 coins that lasts for very long.

Theoretically, it takes a progressive jackpot of 8,700 coins for this game to reach a potential Payback of 100%. It is doubtful that such a payoff level has ever been reached in the entire history of Video Poker.

When you see a crowded bank of progressive machines that has reached a high jackpot level, it is interesting to note that the knowledgeable players invariably cash out and quit playing as soon as someone hits the jackpot. Without the big payoff, the Payback Percentage on most progressive machines is usually lousy. This game is no exception.

For the most part, the best play tactics, as shown on Tables 4-10a and 4-10b, are about the same as with the standard Full Pay Jacks or Better

Fundamental rules include:
Never hold a kicker.
Never draw to an inside straight.
With 3 unsuited high cards, do not hold the ace.

With the 8-5 Progressive game, it is marginally better to hold three cards to a royal flush rather than a high pair.

With the nominal Payback Percentage below 98%, the 8-5 Jack or Better Video Poker game is hardly worth playing.

To repeat the caveat given for the previous turkey: Unless the casino is offering some special inducement to play this particular game, or it is the instrument in a tournament of some sort, you should avoid it. Find something else.

Double Double Bonus Video Poker

Double Double Bonus Video Poker is the last in the listings of playable Video Poker games. With its Theoretical Payback of only 97.8%, it wouldn't be worth considering except that the darn things are everywhere. It is obvious why the casinos love them. Most players seem to be roped in by the big bonuses for the Four of a Kinds as shown on Table 4-11c. The low payoffs for the little hands account for the lousy Payback Percentage.

Table 4-11c

Double Double Bonus Video Poker Pay Table 97.8% Payback					
	1 Coin	2 Coins	3 Coins	4 Coins	5 Coins
Royal Flush	250	500	750	1000	4000
Straight Flush	50	100	150	200	250
Four Aces	160	320	480	640	800
with 2 3 or 4	400	800	1200	1600	2000
Four 2s 3s 4s	80	160	240	320	400
with A 2 3 or 4	160	320	480	640	800
Four 5s - Ks	50	100	150	200	250
Full House	9	18	27	36	45
Flush	5	10	15	20	25
Straight	4	8	12	16	20
3 of a Kind	3	6	9	12	15
Two Pair	1	2	3	4	5
Jacks or Better	1	2	3	4	5

The popularity of the Double Double game makes it a frequent subject of casino tournaments and various local promotions. Consequently, it is be helpful to know how to play it correctly. Unfortunately with most tournaments and promotions the amount of play is so limited that skill usually accounts for less than speed. Therefore, spending the time to learn the intricacies of the best play, as shown on Tables 4-11a and 4-11b, is questionable.

Nonetheless, since the game is basically a Jacks or Better game, the same fundamental rules apply, with a few notable exceptions. The high bonuses actually justify making plays that normally would only be made based on hunches or high alcohol content.

For example, with a full house containing three aces, the mathematics justify discarding the low pair from a full house (lines 5 and 6 on Table 4-11a). The same applies to Two Pair that contain a Pair of Aces (lines 12, 13 and 14). Also, if a hand contains two high cards with one of them an ace, it is best to hold only the ace.

Although it may be tempting to keep a 2, 3, or 4 kicker with Three Aces, it is not justified by the probabilities; nor it is correct to keep a kicker with a low Three of a Kind.

With Double Double Bonus, holding a 4 card inside straight is marginally better than drawing 5 cards.

On a 25¢ Double Double Bonus Video Poker machine, at the standard 500 hands per hour with the resulting $650 in play action, the nominal loss rate is $13.75 per hour. That presumes, of course that you play long enough to get your share of the Bonus Four of Kinds. If you don't, or if you are just having a bad session, this game can be brutal.

The Theoretical 97.8% Payback for Double Double Bonus Video Poker puts it in the range of the almost, but not quite playable unless they are giving away money, category. There are better games than this one.

Miscellaneous Promotional Games

In addition to Baccarat, Craps, Pai Gow, High Payback Slots and the Medium Payback Video Poker games, there are usually a number of new or promotional games that can have a Payback Percentage that puts them in the range of the playable, if they are played skillfully enough and if the casino is providing significant comp value. Some of the current offerings include: Spanish Blackjack, Super-Fun 21 and Catch a Wave.

With Spanish Blackjack, which is a Blackjack game with liberal rules to make up for removing the 10's from the deck, the House Percentage, depending on the specific house rules can vary from about 0.4% to 0.8% with the best basic strategy employed. If you don't play according to the best play basic strategy or if the house rules aren't quite up to snuff, then you are ripe for plucking.

Super-Fun 21 is another promotional Blackjack variety that offers very liberal rules to make up for only paying 1 to 1 for a Blackjack. The House Percentage, if the game is played correctly is a shade under 1%.

The best play tactics for Spanish Blackjack, Super-Fun 21 and Catch a Wave can be found on Michael Shakelford's excellent web site: wizardofodds.com.

It takes a real sense of adventure to risk playing a new game. You need to be very careful about the various new and promotional games out there. There is usually some sort of catch. The house rules and percentages vary from casino to casino and, in some instances, from day to day. Needless to say, the changes are seldom favorable to the players. It only makes good sense to do your homework before risking your money.

Occasionally casinos can make a mistake and offer a game that gives the players a better deal than was intended. After all, nobody's perfect. I have seen two prime examples.

In one case, at the Four Queens in Las Vegas, there was a mix-up about setting the Pay Table on four Bonus Deuces Wild Video Poker machines. The supervisor had told the technician to set the Pay Tables to make them Full Pay Deuces Wild. He meant to say: Full Pay "Bonus" Deuces Wild. The technician did exactly what he was told and set the Pay Tables for 9-5 Deuces Wild, with extra payoffs for the natural hands that are the characteristic of the Bonus Deuces Wild variety. The Player Percentage on those four machines was a little over 2% for the two weeks or so that they were in play. It was surprising how long they lasted.

Another example occurred a few years ago with a game called: Twist-A-Jack. It was a variety of blackjack that allowed the players to bet on either their player's hand or the dealer's hand, similar to Baccarat. When it was first installed on a Blackjack Table in the Golden Nugget in Las Vegas, it initially looked too good to be true. It was. There was a mistake in the implementation of the rules.

That first evening, a couple of sharp cookies jumped on the game and took it for several thousand dollars during the night. The next morning when the drop box was counted, the flaw in the rules was discovered and it was changed on the spot. By 10 o'clock in the morning when a few potential players, like myself, who had taken too long to figure out that the game could be beaten, came dashing into the casino to cash in, we were too late.

Chapter 5 - The Ugly Games

This category of casino games, the ones for which the House Percentage exceeds about 2%, should be played only when someone, who is serious about it, is holding a gun at your head. Otherwise, only those people who really want to get plucked like a chicken should play these games. Not only are you virtually certain to lose if you play them very much, the House Percentage on these games is high enough to insure that the plucking will occur quite rapidly.

These games include: Keno, both the Bingo-like variety and Video Keno, Big Six Wheel, Roulette, Caribbean Stud Poker, Let it Ride, Three Card Poker, War and all varieties of Slot Machines that don't give you an iron clad guarantee that the House Percentage is 2% or less.

Damon Runyon once said: "It may be that the race is not always to the swift, nor the battle to the strong - but that is the way to bet." These are not the ones to bet on. I cannot emphasize too strongly that you simply should not play these games. Surely somewhere you can find better games than these. To echo Sam Kinison: "Go where the food is."

It amazes me that various gambling experts, the ones who write books anyway, will tell you that you are sure to lose if you play these games then proceed to explain how to play them in great detail. Am I missing something here? It is a lot like someone saying: "If you put your hand in this meat grinder, it will chew it off." Then they continue with: "Now, stand on one foot and hold your hand like this… "

Now, not to be too different, let's take a look at a few of these turkeys.

Keno

Never play Keno with a blood alcohol level of less that 0.20%. Otherwise, when your family and so-called friends infer that you might be stupid, you will always have the fallback position of saying: "Hey, I was drunk."

The House Percentages at Keno, which range from about 15% to 30%, are nearly as bad as the state lotteries and none of the profit goes to support the public schools.

It should be noted that someone needs to calculate and publish the odds from time to time. That's what mathematicians and actuaries are for. But, it tends to add undeserved credence to the game when they talk about the best places to play Keno. It is sort of like discussing the differences between being shot in the head with a .357 magnum or a .44 magnum. It doesn't really matter. You get splattered. Dead is dead. Get with the program, Mike.

Playing Keno is really easy, for obvious reasons. In order to make the game interesting, you first have to get your blood alcohol level up to standard. To get the correct number, divide your hat size by the number of drinks you've had in the last two hours. When the number is smaller than one, you are ready to play.

Then, you obtain a form; from the Keno booth, from a Keno Runner or from any of the 630,000 little stashes around the casino. At the same time, you pick up a crayon.

Keno players are not allowed to possess sharp objects.

Make a mark with your crayon, any kind of mark: an X, a circle, a check mark, an underline, a box, an arrow, a star…

whatever; on any of the numbers, which range from 1 to 80. It doesn't really matter how many numbers you mark; anything from 1 up to 20 or so.

It doesn't even matter if you mark more than 20 because when you hand your form and money to the Keno Clerk or Keno Runner, she will check it over and say something like: "Oh, it looks like you have marked too many numbers. Which ones would you like to delete Sir?

You stare at her blankly. She will smile and say something like: "Well, we'll just take off these last 30 numbers." and hand you a receipt, a Keno ticket.

After a while, someone with a Bingo-like contraption will call out a bunch of numbers, about 20 or so, and the Keno Tote boards all over the casino will light up like it is the Fourth of July with the numbers they called.

First, you stare at one of the Tote boards for a while and then you stare, blankly, at your Keno ticket. Now, you make your move: you stagger over to the Keno Booth, slap your Keno ticket on the counter and ask, in a loud voice: "How much did I win?"

The Keno Clerk will take your ticket, compare it to the flock of numbers they just called and say something like: "I'm sorry Sir, but your ticket isn't a winner. Would you like to play again?"

You stare at her, blankly. Then, after a while, you whip out your trusty crayon and repeat the process until you run out of money.

Big Six Wheel

The turnip truck always goes right by the Big Six Wheel. The folks playing it have just fallen off and are ready to party. Let the good times roll!

All you have to do is walk up to the table in front of the Big Six Wheel and place some money on one of the betting areas, or symbols, which are usually inlaid bills of various denominations. If you don't put up enough money to meet the table minimum bet requirement, the dealer will smile at you condescendingly and will say something like: "I'm sorry sir, but the minimum bet is $1."

Then, you fumble around for a while and find out that the dealer doesn't want to take three quarters, two dimes and a nickel, either. When you finally get your dollar bill down on the $5 symbol, the dealer will say something like: "Any more bets?"

You look at the wheel and notice that there are a lot more $1 possibilities than $5 possibilities. With lightning speed, you bang a dollar bill down on the $1 symbol. Now you're covered. About this time, the dealer will give the wheel a spin. Then, it is your job to blend in with the other players by whooping and making loud spinning noises.

As the wheel slows, the dealer will wave his hand over the table and say something like: "No more bets." You hold your breath as it grinds to a stop and if it doesn't land on one of your symbols, you exhale and groan loudly.

If it should stop on the $1 symbol or $5 symbol, making you a winner, you are supposed to squeal, jump up and down and shout: "I won. I won. I won."

The only good thing about the game I can think of is that it is easy to learn. It goes without saying that it is impossible to beat.

Depending on the payoff schedule, the House Percentage varies from about 10% to 20% or more. From time to time, some consideration is given to techniques known as "Clocking the Wheel" and "Orbital Mechanics". These flights of fancy are discussed in the Roulette section.

Roulette

Sometimes, when your feet are really hurting and you can't find a seat at a decent Blackjack table, you might sit down at a Roulette table. They have nice chairs. I can't think of any other reason to be there. When the dealer or "croupier" offers to sell you some table chips, you should decline the offer since the darn things aren't any good anywhere except on that particular Roulette table.

Supposedly Einstein once said: "The only way to win at roulette is to steal chips from the dealer." It is actually that bad. But, just because Roulette has been around for so long and is so venerated, it has a lot of interesting history and deserves some discussion.

With an American wheel, the house has a 5.26% advantage. There are 38 numbers and you only get paid at 36 for 1. It doesn't matter whether you bet Red or Black; Odd or Even; 1st Half or 2nd Half; 1st, 2nd, or 3rd dozen; 1st, 2nd, or 3rd column; straight up numbers; groups of two, three, four, six; or any combination of the above. The house still has a 5.26% advantage... unless, you bet the group of 5, the numbers 00, 0, 1, 2, and 3. Then, the House Percentage goes up to 7.3%. The best you can do is get 36 for 38.

You don't believe it? Ok, bet every number: 00, 0, and 1 through 36. One of them is bound to hit. You have put out 38 chips. When you get paid off for your winning number and pick up the chip left on the table, you will have exactly 36, which in higher mathematical circles is considered to be a net loss of 2 chips.

Still don't believe it? Bet both Red and Black, 18 chips each, and put a chip on each of the Greens, 0 and 00. You have all the possibilities covered with a mere 38 chips. When you win, which you must, you once again have a to- tal of 36 chips. Again, you have a net loss of 2 chips.

You can do the same thing with the top half and bottom half; the thirds or the columns, just remember to also cover the greens. It doesn't matter how you cut it, slice it, twist it, or turn it. At best, the house only pays back 36 for each 38.

History is replete with tales of Roulette systems. For cen- turies, Roulette has drawn would-be mathematicians like flies to a fresh road-apple. Legitimate mathematicians, too, have taken up the study of the possibilities, but, like Ein- stein, they quickly come to the conclusion that Roulette will soundly beat any system that doesn't involve larceny.

But still, there are a couple of possibilities.

The time-honored method is to "Clock the Wheel". Take enough data on which numbers come up, on which wheels, and eventually you may find a wheel that is flawed enough for you to make your fortune.

A flawed, out of balance, worn Roulette wheel will tend to favor certain numbers. From time to time, the "Clockers" have been said to happen upon one. Look hard enough and you might too.

You don't have to have good enough data to pick the actual number the ball is going to hit. All you have to do is avoid betting the numbers that the ball certainly won't hit. If you can eliminate just two numbers, you will have taken away the House Percentage. Eliminate three, and this Roulette wheel is a plum ready for picking. If you should happen upon such a flawed wheel, it is likely that the house will have it fixed before you hurt them too badly.

Some rocket scientists, with greed in their hearts, have come up with another way: "Orbital Mechanics". It has some merit. Bets may usually be placed until the ball is nearly ready to fall from the track onto the wheel. Theoretically, it is possible to calculate the landing zone of the ball, in a fashion similar to the orbital mechanics of space flight re-entry.

Doing the mathematics requires extensive data and equipment capable of doing precise observation and computation, which are illegal to have in your possession while inside a casino. If you are caught with such hardware, plan on going to jail for a long time.

Sometimes, just sometimes, with just casual observation it may be possible to estimate the landing zone well enough to overcome the house advantage. It takes a good eye and some special conditions. You need a consistent dealer; not a change-up artist or a fumble finger novice, but a smooth professional dealer who keeps the wheel speed constant and throws the ball about the same number of revolutions time after time. With good visual acuity and just the right conditions, it just may be possible.

Knowledge of the terrain is essential for the method to work. The numbers are not randomly placed. Take the American wheel as an example:

The top of the wheel has the three number set: 1 00 27
Next to the top is the first strange set: 10 25 29 12
Then come the regular groups of four: 8 19 31 18
                                              6 21 33 16
                                            4 23 35 14
At the bottom is the other set of three: 2 0 28
Next to the bottom is the other strange set: 9 26 30 11
Then, again, the regular groups of four: 7 20 32 17
                                              5 22 34 15
                                            3 24 36 13

Note that the sequential odd and next even numbers are opposite each other on the wheel. Except for the strange sets, each group of four follows the same pattern: the first and second numbers add up to 27, the first and third numbers add up to 39, and the fourth number is 10 more than the first. Recognizing the regularity can make the number sequence easier to memorize.

European wheels are arranged differently, and give the house a smaller percentage, 2.7% compared to 5.26% for American wheels. But then, you seldom find European wheels in this country. When you do, the house usually insists that dealers work at being unpredictable.

With a regular right-handed American wheel, the wheel is normally turned counter clockwise, and the ball is spun clockwise. At first, the ball speed is so fast that the wheel has barely moved before the ball has whizzed around back to its starting point. Twenty times or so, the ball will lap the track. A really good dealer will have a phenomenal hang time, maybe thirty laps.

As the ball begins to slow down, it will quarter the wheel. That is, the wheel will rotate one-quarter turn for each lap of the ball. Then, the ball will halve the wheel: one lap for each half spin. Finally, the ball speed will slow down to the same speed as the wheel and the ball will lap the wheel so that the ball will meet the same number that it met on the last lap. This is referred to as the precession point; another few laps, then the ball falls from the track.

The ball will probably hit one of the diamond shaped barriers, and skip wildly around and through the pockets (or shoes) until it comes to rest.

If you have a good eye, and a lot of patience, eventually you might see that the ball tends to fall at a fixed distance from the precession point. That is, a fixed distance that depends on: the speed of the wheel, the frictional forces between that particular ball on that particular wheel, how much humidity there is in the air, whether the dealer washed his hands on his last break or recently stuck his finger in his nose, the phase of the moon, and about ten thousand other factors.

If you think of the wheel as the face of a clock, with the precession point at 12 o'clock, then finding out that the ball tends to fall at about 3, 6, 9, or 12 o'clock has the potential to make you very rich.

Working against you is that bloody bounce. The wheel never seems to kick the ball the same way twice. That's also the purpose of the diamond shaped barriers, to add some variety to the bounce.

Finally, once you think that you have discovered the relationship between the precession point and the landing point, there often isn't enough time to bet the numbers. Then, you must learn to recognize the relationship between the half point and the landing zone; or even between the one-quarter point and the landing zone. The problem is that the further back you make the estimate, the wider the scatter will be.

All of this assumes that the house hasn't given some thought to the same thing; that they haven't taken appropriate counter-measures. But rest assured, the casino managers also read the literature out there and have added more bounce to the ball, made wheels with shallower shoes to increase the scatter and have trained the dealers to throw change-ups and frequently diddle the wheel speed.

Evidence that the casinos have worked out appropriate counter-measures is shown by the "Snake-Bets" on some Roulette layouts. Some casinos are so sure the landing zone of the ball can't be effectively estimated that they have relieved the punters of the necessity of memorizing the number sequence. They have printed the wheel number sequence on the felt to encourage the players to bet the actual sequence. All you need to do is plunk down a stack of chips and tell the dealer: "Give me a Snake Bet starting with 4." The dealer will obligingly place the chips on the sequence 4, 23, 35, 14, …

You need to appreciate that casinos have lot of money and know how to use it to protect themselves. For centuries, they have hired experts of all kinds to figure out how to cheat the games like Roulette and then they hired more experts to help them come up with ways to prevent it. Surely you don't think these folks are easy marks.

Every day, Roulette grinds out a healthy profit for the casinos. Every day, they count the drop on every table. If it falls off, even a little, they make sure they understand precisely what happened before they reopen the game for the day's play. They pour over the videotapes of the previous day's action and have a team of technicians go over every aspect of the wheel assembly with precision instruments to check the calibration until they have run the cause to ground and fixed it.

The most important things for you to know about Roulette is that the casinos really, really like the game and you should never, ever play it. Roulette's percentage would grind down the Rock of Gibraltar, in short order.

The Sports Book

Usually sports betting is not a gambling activity; it is a partisan demonstration. Most of the bets at the casino Sports Book have such a strong House Percentage 4.5% to 30% or so, that they are beyond the range of rational wagering. Unless you are in on the fix, you just shouldn't bet on sports.

From time to time, there are a few bets that have a House Percentage that is 2% or less. Money Line bets sometimes come in under the wire. When the difference between what you have to bet on the favorite to win 100 units and what you would win if you bet 100 units on the underdog is 10 units, it is called a 10¢ Money Line and is a marginal bet.

As an example, when the favorite and underdog are listed at –120 and +110, it is a 10¢ Money Line. With the favorite at –120, you have to put up 120 to win 100, and with the underdog at +110, you put up 100 to win 110. The House

Percentages on these two wagers are 1.9% and 2.3%, respectively. At –195 and +185, also a 10¢ Money Line, the House Percentages are 0.9% and 1.7%

There has been a lot of talk about Sports Book Arbitrage: It is a risk-free pair of opposite wagers, at different odds; such that, regardless of the outcome, you make a net profit on the pair of wagers. That's what the bookies are trying to do. Should you find a pair of books with wildly different lines, you could do the same thing, but don't count on it.

Outside of the casino, you might be able to take advantage of the Las Vegas line. Go to the home turf of the underdog and stir up even money bets. If your hospital bills aren't too big, you might be able to show a profit.

Caribbean Stud Poker

Another game the casinos really like is Caribbean Stud Poker. It has a strong House Percentage, like Roulette, of about 5.2%. That's why they like it. Don't play it.

It can be an interesting game to watch, from the sidelines. The most interesting part is trying to figure out why the players just keep on playing while their fortunes steadily diminish. I have heard of people winning at Caribbean Stud Poker, but I have never seen it happen. Oh yeah, they might win a hand or two, here and there. I've even seen a couple players draw big hands and get large payoffs, but they always seem to give it back before they leave.

The game is played by the player first putting up an ante, a preliminary bet. Five cards are dealt to all concerned. One of the dealer's cards is exposed. If the player likes his prospects, he puts up a bet equal to twice his ante. If not, he folds and loses his ante. The dealer then checks out his hand. If it is not an Ace-King or better hand, the dealer folds and just pays off the antes of the players who stayed. The additional wagers are pushed back.

If the dealer has an Ace-King or better hand, it "qualifies" and is compared to each of the surviving players hands. If the dealer's hand is higher than the player's hand, the dealer bags the player's bets. If the player's hand is better than the dealer's hand, the dealer pays off the ante at even money and pays the additional wager according to a Video Poker kind of Pay Table that looks like this:

AK or pair	1 to 1
Two Pair	2 to 1
Three of a Kind	3 to 1
Straight	4 to 1
Flush	5 to 1
Full House	7 to 1
Four of a Kind	20 to 1
Straight Flush	50 to 1
Royal Flush	100 to 1

A little less than half the time, 43.7% to be precise, the dealer's hand will fail to qualify, and the player will win the ante, if he stayed in. Obviously, the player should not stay in if his hand is worse than Ace-King. The player that always stays with a hand of Ace-King or better will be giving the house a Percentage of 5.7%.

If the player always stays with any pair or better, he will be giving the house 5.5%. If the player diddles around, discriminating between various Ace-King hands as a function of the dealer's exposed card, this "optimal strategy" will cut the House Percentage to a mere 5.2%, as if it really mattered.

As if just playing the game wasn't enough of a sucker bet, the casino usually offers another bet, usually a $1 bet, for another schedule of progressive bonus payoffs. If this side bet's progressive payoffs are high enough, the Percentage on it can be favorable to player, but it is never favorable enough to justify playing the game in the first place.

Caribbean Stud is a totally synthetic game; that is, it was made up just to fleece the tourists sometime in the 1980's. It started, as the name implies, in the Caribbean and has spread, like a plague, to most of the legitimate casinos around the world. Apparently, the owners of the game are satisfied with a small enough royalty so that the casinos don't mind sharing the wealth.

Three Card Poker

Three Card Poker is another synthetic game, designed expressly to separate you from your money. The House Percentage is very strong, read: lousy for the players. It varies from 3.4% to 4.3% for the player's three card poker hand against the dealer's hand or from 2.3% to 7.3% for the "Pairplus" side bet, depending on the payout schedules.

Do I really have to say it? (Don't play this turkey.)

Should you decide to kill 5 or 10 minutes watching this game: it is played by the victim first putting up an ante, and if so desired, a side bet to hasten the plucking process. Then, three cards are dealt to each of the participants, including the plucker, I mean the dealer. If the victim likes the prospects of his hand beating the dealer's, he may raise by putting a up another bet, to further hasten the plucking process, or he may just give up and let the dealer have the money he has already put up.

Should the dealer's hand not contain a queen or better, the surviving victims get paid even money for their antes and their raises push. If the dealer's hand does contain a queen or better, then it is compared to the players hands. You know what happens if the dealer's hand is better. If the player's hand is better, then both the ante and the raise are paid at even money, and the ante gets a bonus according to a Video Poker kind of pay table. If the Pairplus side bet contains, as the name implies, a pair or better, then, it too gets a payoff according to, yet again, another Video Poker kind of pay table.

While you are watching this spectacle, you should not stand too near the table. The odor of turnips is very strong.

Let it Ride

Like Caribbean Stud Poker and Three Card Poker, Let it Ride is another game made-up with its express purpose to pluck the unwary. Its House Percentage is a healthy 3.5%. The casinos like it a lot, too. Don't play it, either.

The game gives the impression that some real strategy, on the part of the player, is involved. Three cards are dealt to each of the players who puts up three equal bets in the little circles in front of him. Then, instead of playing against the dealer, the two cards the dealer puts in front of him are community cards. If the player likes his prospects with the three cards dealt to him, he can leave up the bet in his first little circle and "Let It Ride". If not, the player can take back the bet in his first little circle.

After the players have decided on the bets in the first circles, the dealer exposes one of the two community cards.
The players then decide what to do with the bet in their
second circle, Let It Ride or take it back. After that is decided, the dealer turns over the other card and the remaining wagers are paid off according to a schedule like:

Tens or better	1 to 1
Two pair	2 to 1
Three of a kind	3 to 1
Straight	5 to 1
Flush	8 to 1
Full house	11 to 1
Four of a kind	50 to 1
Straight flush	200 to 1
Royal flush	1,000 to 1

There is often a side bet offered for $1 or so which is a
sucker bet of major proportions. The House Percentage is
invariably large enough to choke a horse.

If the player only lets it ride with a hand of Tens or Better
or with a strong draw to a Straight Flush on the first choice
and then relaxes that criteria only to include a strong draw
to a Straight or a Flush on the second choice, he can keep
the House Advantage down to about 3.5%

The player can achieve the optimum 0% House Advantage
if he never puts any money into any of the little circles.

War

Casino War is undoubtedly the dumbest game ever to be
played in a casino. It is like the card game little children
play, but instead of winning each other's cards, you and the

casino try to win each other's money based on the sole criterion of who turns over the highest card.

The casino's edge on the basic game, a surprisingly low but unacceptable 2.3%, derives from the instances of ties, when both the dealer and the player turn over a card of the same value. At that time, the player may elect to give up his wager, or place and additional wager on the outcome of a second try. If the player wins the tiebreaker, he only gets paid off on one bet. If the player loses the tiebreaker, he loses both bets.

Should the whoopers and squealers choose to surrender after an initial tie, the House Percentage goes to 3.7%. If they bet on the possibility of an initial Tie, these sophisticates give the casino an advantage of about 18%.

Next, they are going to offer Slap Jack.

Slot Machines

If you enjoy watching spinning wheels and flashing lights, you would be better off playing in the amusement arcade. It costs less and has better special effects.

Two sets of conditions are necessary before you should even consider playing a slot machine:

1. There should be a sign on the machine, backed up by some competent legal authority, that says this turkey is guaranteed to have a Payback Percentage in excess of 98%, and
2. You have checked in with the casino's Players Club, received a Player's Club Card, have been given firm assurances that significant comps will be authorized for the

*amount of money you have to play with so that all you have
to do is put your Player's Club card into the machine and
feed it your money.*

If these conditions have been met, then this section of this
book does not apply. Read the section in the previous
chapter on High Payback Slots.

If these conditions have not been met, then do not play
these slot machines. If you insist on playing them, stand by
to be plucked.

Instructions: Put your money in the slot and pull the handle
or push the button. Watch the wheels spin and the lights
flash. That's it: end of story. There is nothing left to tell.

Sometimes it gives you some of your money back. Mostly,
it doesn't. How much do you need to know about throwing
your money away?

Low Payback Video Poker

Video Poker machines run the entire gamut from reasonable little plums that you can profitably play to rude bar-
baric pluckers that won't even kiss you first. Unless you
pay close attention to the pay tables, they all rook arike.
Unless you can identify the machine, by its pay table, as
being one of the plums that you know how to play, don't
even consider putting any money anywhere near it.

The following pay tables are the mug shots of the Video
Poker games you should never, ever play. You should note
that tables showing you the best play for these games are
not included. The best play is to not play them.

Table 5-1

Bonus Deuces Video Poker Pay Table 95.3% Payback - Do Not Play					
	1 Coin	2 Coins	3 Coins	4 Coins	5 Coins
Royal Flush	250	500	750	1000	4000
4 Deuces W Ace	400	800	1200	1600	2000
Four Deuces	200	400	600	800	1000
Wild Royal	25	50	75	100	125
Five Aces	80	160	240	320	400
Five 3s,4s,or 5s	40	80	120	160	200
Five 6s-Ks	20	40	60	80	100
Straight Flush	10	20	30	40	50
Four Of A Kind	4	8	12	16	20
Full House	3	6	9	12	15
Flush	2	4	6	8	10
Straight	1	2	3	4	5
3 Of A Kind	1	2	3	4	5

Table 5-2

Bonus Poker Video Poker Pay Table 96.9% Payback - Do Not Play					
	1 Coin	2 Coins	3 Coins	4 Coins	5 Coins
Royal flush	250	500	750	1000	4000
Straight flush	50	100	150	200	250
Four Aces	80	160	240	320	400
Four 2s-4s	40	80	120	160	200
Four 5s-Ks	25	50	75	100	125
Full house	6	12	18	24	30
Flush	5	10	15	20	25
Straight	4	8	12	16	20
3 of a kind	3	6	9	12	15
Two pair	2	4	6	8	10
Jacks or better	1	2	3	4	5

Table 5-3

Bonus Poker Video Poker Pay Table 95.8% Payback - Do Not Play					
	1 Coin	2 Coins	3 Coins	4 Coins	5 Coins
Royal flush	250	500	750	1000	4000
Straight flush	50	100	150	200	250
Four Aces	80	160	240	320	400
Four 2s-4s	40	80	120	160	200
Four 5s-Ks	25	50	75	100	125
Full house	10	20	30	40	50
Flush	8	16	24	32	40
Straight	6	12	18	24	30
3 of a kind	3	6	9	12	15
Two pair	1	2	3	4	5
Jacks or better	1	2	3	4	5

Table 5-4

Bonus Poker Deluxe Video Poker Pay Table 96.3% Payback - Do Not Play					
	1 Coin	2 Coins	3 Coins	4 Coins	5 Coins
Royal Flush	250	500	750	1000	4000
Straight Flush	50	100	150	200	250
4 of a Kind	80	160	240	320	400
Full House	7	14	21	28	35
Flush	5	10	15	20	25
Straight	4	8	12	16	20
3 of a Kind	3	6	9	12	15
Two Pair	1	2	3	4	5
Jacks or Better	1	2	3	4	5

Table 5-5

Bonus Poker Deluxe Video Poker Pay Table 95.4% Payback - Do Not Play					
	1 Coin	2 Coins	3 Coins	4 Coins	5 Coins
Royal Flush	250	500	750	1000	4000
Straight Flush	50	100	150	200	250
4 of a Kind	80	160	240	320	400
Full House	6	12	18	24	30
Flush	5	10	15	20	25
Straight	4	8	12	16	20
3 of a Kind	3	6	9	12	15
Two Pair	1	2	3	4	5
Jacks or Better	1	2	3	4	5

Table 5-6

Deuces Wild Video Poker Pay Table 97.6% Payback - Do Not Play					
	1 Coin	2 Coins	3 Coins	4 Coins	5 Coins
Royal Flush	250	500	750	1000	4000
Four Deuces	200	400	600	800	1000
Wild Royal	20	40	60	80	100
5 of a Kind	12	24	36	48	60
Straight Flush	10	20	30	40	50
4 of a Kind	4	8	12	16	20
Full House	4	8	12	16	20
Flush	3	6	9	12	15
Straight	2	4	6	8	10
3 of a Kind	1	2	3	4	5

Table 5-7

Deuces Wild Video Poker Pay Table 96.8% Payback - Do Not Play				
	1 Coin	2 Coins	3 Coins	4 Coins	5 Coins
Royal Flush	250	500	750	1000	4000
Four Deuces	200	400	600	800	1000
Wild Royal	25	50	75	100	125
5 of a Kind	16	32	48	64	80
Straight Flush	13	26	39	52	65
4 of a Kind	4	8	12	16	20
Full House	3	6	9	12	15
Flush	2	4	6	8	10
Straight	2	4	6	8	10
3 of a Kind	1	2	3	4	5

Table 5-8

Deuces Wild Video Poker Pay Table 94.3% Payback - Do Not Play				
	1 Coin	2 Coins	3 Coins	4 Coins	5 Coins
Royal Flush	250	500	750	1000	4000
Four Deuces	200	400	600	800	1000
Wild Royal	25	50	75	100	125
5 of a Kind	15	30	45	60	75
Straight Flush	9	18	27	36	45
4 of a Kind	4	8	12	16	20
Full House	3	6	9	12	15
Flush	2	4	6	8	10
Straight	2	4	6	8	10
3 of a Kind	1	2	3	4	5

Table 5-9

Double Bonus Video Poker Pay Table				
96.4% Payback - Do Not Play				
	1 Coin	2 Coins	3 Coins	4 Coins	5 Coins
Royal Flush	250	500	750	1000	4000
Four Aces	160	320	480	640	800
Four 2s, 3s, or 4s	80	160	240	320	400
Four 5s thru Ks	50	100	150	200	250
Straight Flush	50	100	150	200	250
Full House	9	18	27	36	45
Flush	6	12	18	24	30
Straight	4	8	12	16	20
3 of a Kind	3	6	9	12	15
Two Pair	1	2	3	4	5
Jacks or Better	1	2	3	4	5

Table 5-10

Double Bonus Video Poker Pay Table				
93.1% Payback - Do Not Play				
	1 Coin	2 Coins	3 Coins	4 Coins	5 Coins
Royal Flush	250	500	750	1000	4000
Four Aces	160	320	480	640	800
Four 2s, 3s, or 4s	80	160	240	320	400
Four 5s thru Ks	50	100	150	200	250
Straight Flush	50	100	150	200	250
Full House	7	14	21	28	35
Flush	5	10	15	20	25
Straight	4	8	12	16	20
3 of a Kind	3	6	9	12	15
Two Pair	1	2	3	4	5
Jacks or Better	1	2	3	4	5

Table 5-11

Double Double Bonus Video Poker Pay Table				
96.8% Payback - Do Not Play				
	1 Coin	2 Coins	3 Coins	4 Coins	5 Coins
Royal Flush	250	500	750	1000	4000
Straight Flush	50	100	150	200	250
Four Aces	160	320	480	640	800
with 2 3 or 4	400	800	1200	1600	2000
Four 2s 3s 4s	80	160	240	320	400
with A 2 3 or 4	160	320	480	640	800
Four 5s - Ks	50	100	150	200	250
Full House	8	16	24	32	40
Flush	5	10	15	20	25
Straight	4	8	12	16	20
3 of a Kind	3	6	9	12	15
Two Pair	1	2	3	4	5
Jacks or Better	1	2	3	4	5

Table 5-12

Double Double Bonus Video Poker Pay Table				
94.7% Payback - Do Not Play				
	1 Coin	2 Coins	3 Coins	4 Coins	5 Coins
Royal Flush	250	500	750	1000	4000
Straight Flush	50	100	150	200	250
Four Aces	160	320	480	640	800
with 2 3 or 4	400	800	1200	1600	2000
Four 2s 3s 4s	80	160	240	320	400
with A 2 3 or 4	160	320	480	640	800
Four 5s - Ks	50	100	150	200	250
Full House	6	12	18	24	30
Flush	5	10	15	20	25
Straight	4	8	12	16	20
3 of a Kind	3	6	9	12	15
Two Pair	1	2	3	4	5
Jacks or Better	1	2	3	4	5

Table 5-13

Jacks or Better Video Poker Pay Table 97.3% Payback - Do Not Play					
	1 Coin	2 Coins	3 Coins	4 Coins	5 Coins
Royal Flush	250	500	750	1000	4000
Straight Flush	50	100	150	200	250
4 of a Kind	25	50	75	100	125
Full House	8	16	24	32	40
Flush	5	10	15	20	25
Straight	4	8	12	16	20
3 of a Kind	3	6	9	12	15
Two Pair	2	4	6	8	10
Jacks or Better	1	2	3	4	5

Table 5-14

Jacks or Better Video Poker Pay Table 96.1% Payback - Do Not Play					
	1 Coin	2 Coins	3 Coins	4 Coins	5 Coins
Royal Flush	250	500	750	1000	4000
Straight Flush	50	100	150	200	250
4 of a Kind	25	50	75	100	125
Full House	7	14	21	28	35
Flush	5	10	15	20	25
Straight	4	8	12	16	20
3 of a Kind	3	6	9	12	15
Two Pair	2	4	6	8	10
Jacks or Better	1	2	3	4	5

Table 5-15

Jacks or Better Video Poker Pay Table					
95.0% Payback - Do Not Play					
	1 Coin	2 Coins	3 Coins	4 Coins	5 Coins
Royal Flush	250	500	750	1000	4000
Straight Flush	50	100	150	200	250
4 of a Kind	25	50	75	100	125
Full House	6	12	18	24	30
Flush	5	10	15	20	25
Straight	4	8	12	16	20
3 of a Kind	3	6	9	12	15
Two Pair	2	4	6	8	10
Jacks or Better	1	2	3	4	5

Table 5-16

Joker Wild Video Poker Pay Table					
96.4% Payback - Do Not Play					
	1 Coin	2 Coins	3 Coins	4 Coins	5 Coins
Royal Flush	250	500	750	1000	4000
5 of a Kind	200	400	600	800	1000
Wild Royal	100	200	300	400	500
Straight Flush	50	100	150	200	250
4 of a Kind	15	30	45	60	75
Full House	7	14	21	28	35
Flush	5	10	15	20	25
Straight	3	6	9	12	15
3 of a Kind	2	4	6	8	10
Two Pair	1	2	3	4	5
Kings or Better	1	2	3	4	5

Table 5-17

Joker Wild Video Poker Pay Table 93.3% Payback - Do Not Play					
	1 Coin	2 Coins	3 Coins	4 Coins	5 Coins
Royal Flush	250	500	750	1000	4000
5 of a Kind	250	500	750	1000	1250
Wild Royal	150	300	450	600	750
Straight Flush	50	100	150	200	250
4 of a Kind	12	24	36	48	60
Full House	6	12	18	24	30
Flush	5	10	15	20	25
Straight	3	6	9	12	15
3 of a Kind	2	4	6	8	10
Two Pair	1	2	3	4	5
Kings or Better	1	2	3	4	5

Table 5-18

Joker Wild Video Poker Pay Table 91.0% Payback - Do Not Play					
	1 Coin	2 Coins	3 Coins	4 Coins	5 Coins
Royal Flush	250	500	750	1000	4000
5 of a Kind	200	400	600	800	1000
Wild Royal	100	200	300	400	500
Straight Flush	50	100	150	200	250
4 of a Kind	10	20	30	40	50
Full House	7	14	21	28	35
Flush	5	10	15	20	25
Straight	3	6	9	12	15
3 of a Kind	2	4	6	8	10
Two Pair	1	2	3	4	5
Kings or Better	1	2	3	4	5

Table 5-19

Super Double Bonus Video Poker Pay Table 96.9% Payback - Do Not Play					
	1 Coin	2 Coins	3 Coins	4 Coins	5 Coins
Royal Flush	250	500	750	1000	4000
Four Aces	160	320	480	640	800
Four Js thru Ks	120	240	360	480	600
Four 2s, 3s, or 4s	80	160	240	320	400
Four 5s thru 10s	50	100	150	200	250
Straight Flush	80	160	240	320	400
Full House	6	12	18	24	30
Flush	5	10	15	20	25
Straight	4	8	12	16	20
3 of a Kind	3	6	9	12	15
Two Pair	1	2	3	4	5
Jacks or Better	1	2	3	4	5

Table 5-20

Tens or Better Video Poker Pay Table 97.9% Payback - Do Not Play					
	1 Coin	2 Coins	3 Coins	4 Coins	5 Coins
Royal Flush	250	500	750	1000	4000
Straight Flush	50	100	150	200	250
4 of a Kind	25	50	75	100	125
Full House	6	12	18	24	30
Flush	5	10	15	20	25
Straight	4	8	12	16	20
3 of a Kind	3	6	9	12	15
Two Pair	2	4	6	8	10
Tens or Better	1	2	3	4	5

Chapter 6 – Winning Systems

If you think that you have a System, or even think that there is a System out there somewhere, that is a sure-fire winner, then burn this book. Otherwise, you are in for a rude shock.

What I mean by a Winning System is some tricky way of placing a series of bets that is intended to, and will insure, that you come out ahead. Are you ready for this? There is no such thing. There never was. There never will be. It is a theoretical impossibility. There is no System that will work; not in this dimension of this universe, anyway.

It has been proven, mathematically, that there is no way of placing a series of bets that will change the House Percentage one single iota. Mathematicians have been re-proving it and trying to explain it for centuries. Enthusiastic non-believers keep bugging them with the same old question: "But suppose you start with…" The mathematicians continue to explain until they collectively turn blue in the face.

Yet, hordes of non-believers keep falling out of the trees with sure-fire Winning Systems in hand ready to do battle with those close-minded mathematicians. Meanwhile, in the background the casino managers are smiling and whispering: "Here, kitty-kitty."

I find it amusing that the advocates of various systems are willing to sell their systems to select members of the general public for only a small fee. But none of them appear to be willing to take their sure-fire, foolproof, can't-be-beat Winning System to a casino, spend their own money and get rich. Now if I had a system that really worked, I wouldn't tell anybody about it, and, just to cover my tracks, I'd write a book saying that it couldn't be done.

Systems, winning or otherwise, are an integral part of gambling. Any manner in which you place your wagers, is actually a system of some kind or another. Flat bets, one chip at a time: one, one, one... ; an arithmetic progression one, two, three, four, five... ; a geometric progression one, two, four, eight... ; ascending; descending; alternating; duplex; complex; simple; compound... The possibilities are virtually endless.

Betting systems tend to fall into two categories: Those that are truly dumb and dangerous, like the Martingale System, and those that are superficially suicidal. For the first case, you risk one big loss to gain a number of small wins. For the second, you risk a number of small losses for one big win. Neither category affects the House Percentage a whit, but both will give the House Percentage multiple whacks at your bankroll.

The Martingale System

The classic Martingale System simply consists of doubling up your wager following every loss. When you win, you win one unit. When you lose you bet twice as many units. If you lose again, you double your wager again and ultimately when you finally win a wager, you come out ahead by one unit. Sounds simple, a sure thing, right?

The Martingale System has been around for a long time. It pre-dates the invention of probability and statistics. Some caveman gambler, somewhere, who first came up with this system undoubtedly thought he had invented the ultimate Winning System.

At first glance, the Martingale System is pretty solid. If you have a big enough bankroll, you will be very hard to beat. Even in this day and age, you can always find someone cheerfully playing it, sure that they are on their way to a fortune.

Consider what happens if you win your first bet: you take back a unit, and bet one unit on the next play. As long as you continue to win, your bankroll simply gains one unit per win. When you walk away after winning 10 bets in a row, you win 10 chips. For a series of wins, there is no difference between the Martingale System and a series of Flat Bets.

But, take a look on Table 6-1 at what happens when you lose a bunch of hands in a row, then, ultimately win one. Sooner or later you've got to win one. Right?

Table 6-1						
Martengale System Assume any number of consecutive losses, ending in a win						
Play Number	Amount from Bankroll	Total Wager	Outcome of Wager	Amount on Table	Amount to Bankroll	Net Win
1	-1	1	-	0	0	-1
2	-2	2	-	0	0	-3
3	-4	4	-	0	0	-7
4	-8	8	-	0	0	-15
5	-16	16	-	0	0	-31
6	-32	32	-	0	0	-63
7	-64	64	-	0	0	-127
8	-128	128	-	0	0	-255
9	-256	256	-	0	0	-511
10	-512	512	-	0	0	-1023
n	n^2	n^2	+	$2n^2$	$2n^2$	1

No matter how many consecutive losses you suffer, sooner or later you must win one. No string of losses can go on forever. Right? After even a bunch of losses in a row, when you ultimately win just one lousy bet, you come out ahead by one unit. You can't lose. Right? If you had been making Flat-Bets: you would have lost a bunch minus one.

Also note the sequence of the numbers in the Total Wager column: 1, 2, 4, 8, 16... This power of two sequence just keeps popping up. After doubling 10 times the number is 1,024. After doubling 20 times, it is 1,048,576.

On looking at Table 6-1, you might say to yourself; "Why is this idiot fooling around displaying all those columns for such a simple example?" Let me say this about that: When you are examining Systems you have to be very careful to account for every chip. More than once, I have seen explanations of Systems in which that chip in the upper left hand corner of the chart, the one you take from your Bankroll to start with, has been assumed to come from nowhere. If you don't watch closely, chips left on the table for the next play, which have been won but not pocketed, will be counted twice.

It is sort of like that old recipe for making chicken soup that starts off: "First you steal a chicken..." These things can get very complicated very quickly. The hand can be a lot quicker than the eye, and all that. If you aren't really careful, before you know it you can begin to compound and multiply those stolen chickens. That kind of examination can make almost any system look like a Winning System.

Before things get complicated let's take a minute and examine the layout of these System Tables, since it is important to not get snookered by some fast talker who is trying to sell you a bum system. The table layout, row by row, follows the action just as it occurs, if you read left to right, play by play. You walk up to the table (any game that pays one for one) at Play Number 1, take 1 unit out of your Bankroll (Amount from Bankroll), put it on the table (Total Wager), win or lose the bet (Outcome of Wager, + or -), observe the pay off (Amount on Table): which will be two if you won and zero if you lost on the first play, if there is anything on the table, you decide how much to take back and put in your poke (Amount to Bankroll). Then and only then do you compute how much you won or lost (Net Win).

It is not kosher to count the chips you leave on the table, at risk, as won chips. You haven't won the units until you pull them out of play and put them in your bankroll. You cannot play your money and have it at the same time. Money at risk is not won money. If you think it is, I have this bridge you might be interested in.

Now, take a look at Table 6-2, where there is a series with

Table 6-2						
Martengale System Assume 4 wins 6 losses, any order, ending in a win						
Play Number	Amount from Bankroll	Total Wager	Outcome of Wager	Amount on Table	Amount to Bankroll	Net Win
1	-1	1	+	2	1	0
2	0	1	+	2	1	1
3	0	1	-	0	0	1
4	-2	2	-	0	0	-1
5	-4	4	+	8	7	2
6	0	1	-	0	0	2
7	-2	2	-	0	0	0
8	-4	4	-	0	0	-4
9	-8	8	-	0	0	-12
10	-16	16	+	32	32	4

4 wins and 6 losses. The effect is that you win 4 units. Flat betting this series of wins and losses would have lost 2 units. So long as you end the series on a win, it doesn't even matter what the order of the wins and losses are, you win four units. The Martingale System always comes out ahead by one unit for every win in a sequence of wagers. What a deal!

There is, however, a fly in the ointment; two flies, actually. Well, they are a lot more like alligators, big hungry alligators. Sooner or later, one or the other of them will devour anyone who takes the Martingale System seriously.

The first problem is that little business about, sooner or later, having to win just one bet. It doesn't take all that many losses in a row before most people run out of money. Go back and take a look at Table 6-1. With just 10 losses in a row, you are into it by over $1,000 to chase one buck. When we get down to real money and not just artificial units, it gets serious, fast. With 20 losses in a row, your investment to bring home that measly $1 would be well over one million.

And it will happen. Sooner or later, everyone runs into a long streak of losses. If you happen to be playing a Martingale System at the time, you can bend over, put your head between your legs... I know whereof I speak. At one time, I lost 22 hands of Blackjack in a row. I didn't make any mistakes. The dealer wasn't cheating; actually he was a friend of mine. I just flat-out lost 22 in a row.

The other problem with the Martingale System is that the casinos don't like to see their valued customers lose a whole bunch on such a silly system. So, they always have this thing called: the Table Limit. It decreases the number of plays, and the amount of bankroll, that it takes to make you a sure loser.

Take for example, a table limit of 500 units and look again at Table 6-1. By the 10th play your necessary wager of 512 units exceeds the 500 unit limit; so you can only bet 500 on the 10th play, thereby locking in a 12 unit loss for the series. To keep from losing the 500, you are then caught in a series of Flat-Bets of 500 units each. And so it goes...

The Martingale System is still tempting at times though. If you have a very large bankroll, in comparison to the unit bet size, and a lot of hair on your chest, you can regularly pick up several of those little units. That assumes that the loss you will suffer if the table limit is reached won't seriously wound your bankroll.

No less than the renowned mathematician Dr. Thorp has pointed out that the probability the cycle will end on or before the 10th turn is 0.9,984; that is, there is only a 0.16% or about one chance in 613 that the 11th turn will be reached. He also points out that if the system is used long enough, it will happen. (Dr. Edward O. Thorp. The Mathematics of Gambling, Lyle Stuart, Inc., Secaucus, N.J., 1984, p. 115)

Fairly often you will see a player go "on tilt", lose control, and start chasing his losses by doubling up; another mani-festation of the Martingale System. It works just well enough, just often enough, to make it really dangerous. After coming back from the edge of disaster, being saved from a loss, repeatedly, some players fall into the habit of chasing their losses by doubling up even though they know that the Martingale System is a recipe for disaster.

Just recently, I saw it happen, again. A young man began pulling $100 bills out of his wallet to chase a sudden losing streak and, within a few more losses, he became quiet and then said softly, to no one in particular: "I just lost all my money." Then, he got up from the table and walked out the door, with a sort of a dazed look about him.

It just breaks my heart to see something like that happen. Few things in the casino are sadder than seeing someone lose the rent money, particularly when it is you. The price, in terms of both money and emotional distress, is enormous. Taint worth it. Don't do it. Listen to someone who has been there: If you seriously fool around with the Martingale System, it will bring you to grief.

The D'Alembert System

The D'Alembert System, alias the Pyramid System, also calls for increasing your wager each time you lose a hand, but, you only increase your bet by one unit each time you lose, and, when you win, you decrease your bet by one unit.

What the D'Alembert System has going for it, besides being simple to understand and put into practice, is that it doesn't require as big a bankroll and won't bust you as quickly. The arithmetic progression, rather than geometric progression, just isn't as dramatic. It is a slower, gentler sort of poison.

Table 6-3 shows the effect of suffering a series of losses with this system. You don't put as much at risk as quickly as you do with the Martingale System, but when you finally win one, you don't come out ahead, either.

This sequence of losses results in a net loss of 44 units. Making Flat-Bets the player would have lost only 9 units. Using the Martingale System would have resulted in a net win of one unit.

Table 6-3						
D'Alembert System						
Assume 10 consecutive losses, then a win						
Play Number	Amount from Bankroll	Total Wager	Outcome of Wager	Amount on Table	Amount to Bankroll	Net Win
1	-1	1	-	0	0	-1
2	-2	2	-	0	0	-3
3	-3	3	-	0	0	-6
4	-4	4	-	0	0	-10
5	-5	5	-	0	0	-15
6	-6	6	-	0	0	-21
7	-7	7	-	0	0	-28
8	-8	8	-	0	0	-36
9	-9	9	-	0	0	-45
10	-10	10	-	0	0	-55
11	-11	11	+	22	22	-44

Starting with a long series of wins, the D'Alembert System is just like Flat-Betting; you come out ahead one unit for each win, until you have a loss, and then you increase your bet from one to two units. That initial loss makes the D'Alembert System look a lot like the Martingale System if it is followed by a choppy win-loss sequence.

Table 6-4 shows a sequence of wins and losses that is a lot less radical than a long series of consecutive wins or consecutive losses. It assumes a sequence made up of 1 win, 2 losses, 2 wins, 3 losses, 3 wins then a loss for a total of 6 wins and 8 losses. It is not an uncommon kind of run.

Most players will probably complain about the string of 5 consecutive losses though.

	Table 6-4					
	D'Alembert System					
	Assume 1 win, 2 losses, 2 wins, 5 losses, 1 win, 1 loss, then 2 wins					
Play Number	Amount from Bankroll	Total Wager	Outcome of Wager	Amount on Table	Amount to Bankroll	Net Win
1	-1	1	+	2	1	0
2	0	1	-	0	0	0
3	-2	2	-	0	0	-2
4	-3	3	+	6	4	-1
5	0	2	+	4	3	2
6	0	1	-	0	0	2
7	-2	2	-	0	0	0
8	-3	3	-	0	0	-3
9	-4	4	-	0	0	-7
10	-5	5	-	0	0	-12
11	-6	6	+	12	7	-11
12	0	5	-	0	0	-11
13	-6	6	+	12	7	-10
14	0	5	+	10	10	0

What the D'Alembert System does, why it can appear to work, is that it forces you to play for higher and higher stakes when you are losing. It is the same sort of idea that is behind the Martingale System. That way, if you are betting more and finally catch a win or two, you get caught up quicker.

The question is: "If you could afford to bet more, why wouldn't you do so from the beginning to give yourself a chance to win more?"

The Fibonacci Series System (Two Win Variation)

There are some really lovely mathematics that touch on numerical manifestations in the physical universe. The Fibonacci Series is a prime example of a set of numbers that is almost magical. It is not surprising, therefore, that it has been worked into a number of Winning Systems.

Let's start with one of the Fibonacci Systems that has the characteristic that you bet more to win less, Table 6-5:

Table 6-5						
The Fibonacci Series System						
Assume 10 consecutive losses, then two wins						
Play Number	Amount from Bankroll	Total Wager	Outcome of Wager	Amount on Table	Amount to Bankroll	Net Win
1	-1	1	-	0	0	-1
2	-1	1	-	0	0	-2
3	-2	2	-	0	0	-4
4	-3	3	-	0	0	-7
5	-5	5	-	0	0	-12
6	-8	8	-	0	0	-20
7	-13	13	-	0	0	-33
8	-21	21	-	0	0	-54
9	-34	34	-	0	0	-88
10	-55	55	-	0	0	-143
11	-89	89	+	178	34	-198
12	0	144	+	288	288	90

It goes like this: After the second play, if you haven't won two in a row, bet two, then, with each subsequent loss increase your bet so that it is equal to the sum of the preceding two bets. The sequence is: 1, 1, 2, 3, 5, 8, 13, 21, 34, 55... With this variation of the system, you continue in this fashion until you win two in a row; then you start over.

When you finally win two in a row, not only do you get even, you come out ahead; 90 units, in this case. The weird part of this system is that if you had simply won 12 in a row you would have come out ahead by only 12 units rather than 90. At first glance, it appears that you win more by losing more. You have to go over the numbers several times to convince yourself that this system really does shine when you are taking a beating in terms of repeated losses. It just don't seem right, somehow.

Now take a look at Table 6-6, at what this Fibonacci Series System does with the same sequence of wins and losses

Table 6-6						
The Fibonacci Series System						
Assume 1 win, 2 losses, 2 wins, 5 losses, 1 win, 1 loss, then 2 wins						
Play Number	Amount from Bankroll	Total Wager	Outcome of Wager	Amount on Table	Amount to Bankroll	Net Win
1	-1	1	+	2	1	0
2	0	1	-	0	0	0
3	-2	2	-	0	0	-2
4	-3	3	+	6	1	-4
5	0	5	+	10	9	5
6	0	1	-	0	0	5
7	-1	1	-	0	0	4
8	-2	2	-	0	0	2
9	-3	3	-	0	0	-1
10	-5	5	-	0	0	-6
11	-8	8	+	16	3	-11
12	0	13	-	0	0	-11
13	-21	21	+	42	8	-24
14	0	34	+	68	68	44

that we considered previously: 1 win, 2 losses, 2 wins, 5 losses, 1 win, 1 loss, then 2 wins.

Are we really cooking or what? Before, when we had this same sequence of wins and losses using the D'Alembert System we could only squeak out with a break–even. The Martingale System would have only brought in a net win of 6 units for the same sequence. Is this Fibonacci Series System really the Golden Goose?

Before you cash in your stocks and bonds, get the deed to the ranch out of the safety deposit box and break the kids' piggy banks, take a moment to reflect. The old adage holds: If it looks too good to be true, it probably is.

This Fibonacci Series System is a prime example. For a few plays, it always looks good on paper. You can check out a lot of short sequences like that shown on Table 6-6 without finding an example that even suggests that there might be a problem, but you can be sure that there is something rotten somewhere. Try running some longer series of trials. You don't want to quit before you have made a fortune, do you?

Just making a few quick calculations indicates that, without a table limit to contend with, you probably can't beg, borrow or steal enough money to bankroll this Fibonacci Series System. If you don't get two wins in a row, by the 20th play your wager would be 6,765 units. To survive 20 consecutive losses you need a bankroll of 17,710 units. For 30, you need 2,178,308. For 40, you need over 268 hundred million.

Ok, now we know the worst. My curiosity got the best of me and I decided ask my computer to estimate the average outcome and bankroll size it would take to make say 20 plays and then flee. Since the worst that could happen would be to lose 17,710 units, maybe it wouldn't be so bad.

After much fumbling around, with a set of 20 plays 100 times, the average Net Win was actually a loss of 138 units; meaning you would have lost 13,800 units in total. (My computer was having a bad day.) The really bad news though was that it required a session bankroll of 10,942 units, indicating that you would need to have the theoretical max of 17,710 units at the ready each time you played.

Re-sorting through the numbers, this time taking into account a table limit of 500 units, did shed a little new light on the situation. With a 500 unit table limit, the average loss was only 8 units and the worst whuppin' was only a mere 3,483 units.

While these results may not be mathematically rock-solid, since the sample size of 100 sessions of 20 plays is a bit small, the results are indicative. You can begin to get an idea of the magnitude of the beast and a new appreciation for the effect of table limits.

My computer tells me (and I have learned to believe it) that, on the average, it takes about 204 plays for this Two Win Version Fibonacci Series System to bump into a table limit of 500 units and leave you in the lurch. Sometimes you can go for 400 or even 500 plays without stubbing your toe on the table limit. That's a lifetime total of maybe 10 hours on a Blackjack table.

If you are really unlucky you will only make it last for about 15 plays. That's hardly a long enough time for the cocktail waitress to bring you a drink.

The problems with this Fibonacci Series System are just the same ones that you have with the Martingale System or the D'Alembert System: sooner or later you will run into a bad streak that will eat up your bankroll and you, without even spitting out the buttons and zippers.

If you think it is possible to hit a long streak without one win, it is several times more likely you will hit a bad patch without two wins in a row. Sometimes it seems like it can go on forever.

These systems; The Martingale System, The D'Alembert System, and this variation of a Fibonacci Series System; have the similar characteristic of requiring you to bet more and more to chase a loss. There are about a zillion of them out there, like this, that are really dangerous. If you should find yourself considering any system where the amount of money required from your pocket keeps going up and up, run, don't walk, to the nearest exit.

Before we move on to the other kinds of systems, the ones where the players appear intent on giving it back as soon as they win it (that is, going after a few bigger wins by suffering a bunch of small losses), let's take a look a system that has the characteristics of both of the major kinds of systems.

The Fibonacci Series System (Up and Down Variation)

The Up and Down Variation of the Fibonacci Series System sort of straddles the fence between system types. You increase your bets in both directions, losing and winning. You bet the Fibonacci Series for any string of either losses or wins, resetting and starting over after a change of direction. You just keep pressing a streak in any direction.

Take a look at Table 6-7 which exposes this Up and Down Variation to the same sequence of wins and losses we looked at with the other systems: 1 win, 2 losses, 2 wins, 5 losses, 1 win, 1 loss, then 2 wins.

Table 6-7						
The Fibonacci Series System (Up and Down Variation)						
Assume 1 win, 2 losses, 2 wins, 5 losses, 1 win, 1 loss, then 2 wins						
Play Number	Amount from Bankroll	Total Wager	Outcome of Wager	Amount on Table	Amount to Bankroll	Net Win
1	-1	1	+	2	1	0
2	0	1	-	0	0	0
3	-1	1	-	0	0	-1
4	-2	2	+	4	3	0
5	0	1	+	2	1	1
6	0	1	-	0	0	1
7	-1	1	-	0	0	0
8	-2	2	-	0	0	-2
9	-3	3	-	0	0	-5
10	-5	5	-	0	0	-10
11	-8	8	+	16	15	-3
12	0	1	-	0	0	-3
13	-1	1	+	2	1	-3
14	0	1	+	2	2	-1

The one unit loss for this sequence isn't very promising, being only slightly better than flat betting the sequence and losing two. However, the water doesn't appear to get deep very quickly. The most you have to bet, even after 5 consecutive losses, is eight units. Remember that this sequence is for 6 wins and 8 losses.

For a choppy series of wins and losses, this system looks like a bunch of flat-bets, until a streak occurs. Although you still have the potential to lose 17,710 units if you take a hit of 20 straight losses, now you also stand a chance to win 17,710 units if you hit a streak of 20 wins rather than only winning 20 units as with the Two Win Variation.

Most of the action with this system looks like that shown on Table 6-8. It doesn't appear to be very dramatic, but then, what's dramatic all depends on how big a unit is and who is risking it.

Table 6-8						
The Fibonacci Series System (Up and Down Variation)						
Assume 20 plays, short streaks, 9 wins 11 losses						
Play Number	Amount from Bankroll	Total Wager	Outcome of Wager	Amount on Table	Amount to Bankroll	Net Win
1	-1	1	-	0	0	-1
2	-1	1	+	2	1	-1
3	0	1	-	0	0	-1
4	-1	1	+	2	1	-1
5	0	1	-	0	0	-1
6	-1	1	+	2	1	-1
7	0	1	+	2	0	-1
8	0	2	+	4	1	0
9	0	3	-	0	0	0
10	-1	1	-	0	0	-1
11	-1	1	-	0	0	-2
12	-2	2	+	4	3	-1
13	0	1	+	2	1	0
14	0	1	-	0	0	0
15	-1	1	-	0	0	-1
16	-2	2	-	0	0	-3
17	-3	3	+	6	5	-1
18	0	1	-	0	0	-1
19	-1	1	-	0	0	-2
20	-2	2	+	4	4	0

Running the Fibonacci Series System (Up and Down Variation) through my computer, 500 plays to the session for 100 sessions, a total of 50,000 plays, showed it to be relatively tame. After 50,000 plays, it was a push; the average Net Win was 0. The biggest win for a session of 500 hands was 355 units and the worst loss was 335 units.

Even though it theoretically has about as much potential for disaster as the Two Win Variation, after several thousand more hands, the worst loss my computer encountered was 1,083 units. About all I could see that this system accomplishes is to increase the average amount wagered and boost the play action somewhat. Even though it didn't raise its head during my short-terms trials, you can be sure there is a big booger in that bush.

Still, if you really think you can beat the odds by using one of these kinds of systems, go ahead. Give it a whirl. What do you have to lose? Your money, your family, your friends, your self-respect, your sanity...

Minimizing Your Losses - Maximizing Your Profits

To be honest, there are some Not So Dumb Systems, Systems that can be amusing when you are playing an even game or, particularly, when you are playing a game where you have the percentage. As I mentioned earlier, any way you place your bets can be considered to be a system, even flat-betting: one, one, one, one...

Unlike the previous systems where you bet more and more after a loss, the following systems are characterized by betting less after a loss. Normally you cut back to one unit, whatever that may be, and stick with it until the flow changes. Only after a win, or series of wins do you increase your bet size. The general ideal is to minimize your losses and maximize your profits. Basically you focus on trying to play big on the house's money.

You have to remember, though, even the better systems of wagering, which involve betting more when you are winning and less when you are losing, do not change the odds or affect the percentage. They only increase the velocity. Experimenting with Systems, to find a reasonable betting sequence that you can be comfortable with, is not an excuse to separate your bankroll into a bunch of little bets against a house game that has an ugly percentage. Only when the percentage is in your favor should you follow that path.

The essence of systems that call for you to increase your wager when you are winning is embodied by the story of the old-timer who walked into the Horseshoe Casino, in the days when they were flexible about the table limit business, and plunked two dollars on the pass line at the craps table. A winning streak struck and after each win, he would just stack the chips up and let them ride. Soon a crowd began to assemble, as the streak continued ... 7, 8, 9, 10... passes in a row. The chips piled up, higher and higher. The $2 stake just kept growing: ...$2,048, $4,096, $8,192, $16,384 and finally after the 14th pass in a row, with $32,768 stacked up, the shooter seven'd out. As the dealer was dragging in the chips and the old-timer began to walk away, one of the by-standers asked: "How much did you lose?" The old-timer just smiled and said: "Two dollars."

In this day and age the table limit would truncate that sequence in every casino I know of. Even so, you occasionally see someone who appears to be reasonably sober take a run at doubling up until the chips turn pink. With enough chips, they can eventually do it.

Press To The Max Betting System

Putting the table minimum down and trying to turn it into the table maximum is a time-honored tradition, for those with sporting instincts. It's easy. On the first play, wager one unit and if you win, press it up: let it ride. On each successive play, bet the total amount won on the previous wager until the table limit is reached. When the table limit is reached (assuming 500 units) drag (take back or recover) 12 units, and bet 500. Continue to bet the limit; then, when a loss occurs, start over with one unit.

Table 6-9 illustrates the Press To The Max Betting System in its best light: a lot of consecutive wins and no table limit.

Table 6-9						
The Press To The Max Betting System (most aggressive)						
Assume n consecutive wins						
Play Number	Amount from Bankroll	Total Wager	Outcome of Wager	Amount on Table	Amount to Bankroll	Net Win
1	-1	1	+	2	0	-1
2	0	2	+	4	0	-1
3	0	4	+	8	0	-1
4	0	8	+	16	0	-1
5	0	16	+	32	0	-1
6	0	32	+	64	0	-1
7	0	64	+	128	0	-1
8	0	128	+	256	0	-1
9	0	256	+	512	0	-1
10	0	512	+	1024	1024	1023
n	1	n^2	+	$2*n^2$	$2*n^2$	$2*n^2 -1$

Note that you are actually behind; that is, losing; until you pull back some of your chips. When you do, say at the end of the 10th play, you will have won 1,023 units, not 1,024 units. Remember that the game started with you putting up a chip, it is included in what you pull back, if you do so, after the nth play.

This is the arch-type of systems that appear to be suicidal. On the average, if you are going for 10 wins in a row, it will take about 1,024 tries and therefore cost 1,024 units. The up side is that on the average you will win 10 in a row about once in every 1,024 tries and get back 1,024 units. The most notable potential for disaster with this system, as with most systems actually, is in being under-capitalized. If you don't have a bankroll that is big enough, you won't be able to last long enough to break even. But if you do …

There is not much point in illustrating the effect of a string of losses with this system. You just keep betting one unit after each loss. Only after a win do you bet more. The point at which you should quit is entirely up to you and the magnitude of your bankroll. It takes some serious money to have a reasonable chance to win some serious money.

I know a lady pit boss who plays what she calls "seven-out" for amusement. Once a week she takes $50 and goes to the casino across the street from where she works. Usually she plays Blackjack, but any low percentage game will do. She starts by playing $5 a hand. If she wins, she presses the bet until she loses or hits seven wins in a row, which amounts to $640. When She loses a hand, she cuts back to one $5 chip at a time. Once in a while she wins the $640 and then quits playing for the night. Mostly she loses the $50, but she is served free drinks while she plays and the pit boss at that casino always comps her and her date a gourmet dinner.

Linear Drag System

The Linear Drag System tries to make up for the short-coming of the Press To The Max System of having nothing to show for a series of wins. You simply take one chip out of your pile on the table for each win after having doubled up on the first win. Table 6-10 shows what it looks like for a gob of wins with a table limit of 500 units.

Play Number	Amount from Bankroll	Total Wager	Outcome of Wager	Amount on Table	Amount to Bankroll	Net Win
			Table 6-10			
		The Linear Drag System (very aggressive)				
		Assume 500 unit table limit, 14 consecutive wins and quit				
1	-1	1	+	2	0	-1
2	0	2	+	4	1	0
3	0	3	+	6	1	1
4	0	5	+	10	1	2
5	0	9	+	18	1	3
6	0	17	+	34	1	4
7	0	33	+	66	1	5
8	0	65	+	130	1	6
9	0	129	+	258	1	7
10	0	257	+	514	14	21
11	0	500	+	1000	500	521
12	0	500	+	1000	500	1021
13	0	500	+	1000	500	1521
14	0	500	+	1000	1000	2521

This very optimistic scenario is obviously very improbable (1 chance in 16,348), but it illustrates the system. In actual practice, the Linear Drag System is nearly as radical as The Press To The Max System.

When you are having a bad day, this system doesn't make it any better. You need to have groups of 3 wins or more, often, to make this system look good. Consider our old friend, the sequence: 1 win, 2 losses, 2 wins, 5 losses, 1 win, 1 loss, then 2 wins. This sequence is shown on Table 6-11 playing havoc with the Linear Drag System.

Table 6-11						
The Linear Drag System (very aggressive)						
Assume 1 win, 2 losses, 2 wins, 5 losses, 1 win, 1 loss, then 2 wins						
Play Number	Amount from Bankroll	Total Wager	Outcome of Wager	Amount on Table	Amount to Bankroll	Net Win
1	-1	1	+	2	0	-1
2	0	2	-	0	0	-1
3	-1	1	-	0	0	-2
4	-1	1	+	2	0	-3
5	0	2	+	4	1	-2
6	0	3	-	0	0	-2
7	-1	1	-	0	0	-3
8	-1	1	-	0	0	-4
9	-1	1	-	0	0	-5
10	-1	1	-	0	0	-6
11	-1	1	+	2	0	-7
12	0	2	-	0	0	-7
13	-1	1	+	2	0	-8
14	0	2	+	4	4	-4

Remember if you had flat bet this sequence of 6 wins and 8 losses, you would have only come out down 2 rather than down 4 when you decided to escape after the 14th play. Only the double win at the end keeps this session from being a real stinker. The other systems, which I have warned you against, really do handle this sequence of wins and losses quite well in comparison.

This kind of session illustrates the main problem with the systems that try to maximize the profit. You have to be winning to make a profit. When you are losing with a system like this, you are going to have a worse day than if you were just flat betting. You would be much better off staying at home and watching TV. It goes something like this: when you are losing, you are losing. Generally, you can't make very good chicken soup out of chicken manure. (Please do not send me any recipes.)

The choppier the sequence, the fewer the runs, the worse it gets. With systems like this, which double up every initial win, you tend to get one unit further behind for every isolated win compared to flat betting. About the only way the Linear Drag System can really do well is for you to hit a series of wins and then get out quickly, about like the Press To The Max System. Dragging a chip from time to time will keep you in the hunt a while longer though. After all, a little bit of something is better than a lot of nothing.

The Press Then Drag System

The Press Then Drag System is designed to multiply the profit from streaky sessions and minimize the chance for disaster by having you revert to one unit bets after each loss. Basically, you are trying to get some money into your pocket and increase the bet on the table at the same time.

You just double up after each initial win. Leave your profit on the table after that first win. Then, after the second win in a row, you pull back half to your Bankroll, which then leaves you in the black with a bigger bet on the table. You alternately press then drag, as shown on Table 6-12.

Table 6-12						
The Press Then Drag System (aggressive)						
Assume 14 consecutive wins and then quit						
Play Number	Amount from Bankroll	Total Wager	Outcome of Wager	Amount on Table	Amount to Bankroll	Net Win
1	-1	1	+	2	0	-1
2	0	2	+	4	2	1
3	0	2	+	4	0	1
4	0	4	+	8	4	5
5	0	4	+	8	0	5
6	0	8	+	16	8	13
7	0	8	+	16	0	13
8	0	16	+	32	16	29
9	0	16	+	32	0	29
10	0	32	+	64	32	61
11	0	32	+	64	0	61
12	0	64	+	128	64	125
13	0	64	+	128	0	125
14	0	128	+	256	256	381

Again, the sequence of 14 straight wins is just being used to illustrate the system, to give you the idea of what the system looks like in the best possible circumstance. This system has both benefits and disadvantages. It is not a thornless rose.

Note that after the second win in a row, you have a profit in your Bankroll and you are playing on house money. After 4 wins in a row, you are ahead by 5 units and are beating up on the casino with 4 units of their own money. It doesn't get much better than this.

So, the Press Then Drag System can accomplish the purpose: when you are winning, you multiply up your profits at house expense without digging yourself into a hole by chasing losses. If the wins and losses are coming in clumps, this kind of system can actually do quite well. You don't even have to be getting more wins than losses, over-all. You just need to have the wins strung together.

The sequence shown on Table 6-13 makes the point that you can come out ahead during a so-so session, provided that the wins come in clumps.

Table 6-13						
The Press Then Drag System (aggressive)						
Assume a streaky series totaling 9 wins among 5 losses						
Play Number	Amount from Bankroll	Total Wager	Outcome of Wager	Amount on Table	Amount to Bankroll	Net Win
1	-1	1	+	2	0	-1
2	0	2	+	4	2	1
3	0	2	+	4	0	1
4	0	4	+	8	4	5
5	0	4	-	0	0	5
6	-1	1	-	0	0	4
7	-1	1	-	0	0	3
8	-1	1	+	2	0	2
9	0	2	+	4	2	4
10	0	2	+	4	0	4
11	0	4	-	0	0	4
12	-1	1	-	0	0	3
13	-1	1	+	2	0	2
14	0	2	+	4	2	4

If you had flat bet this sequence you would have also won 4 units but then you wouldn't have had the chance to make a break out if only that 6th win in a row had materialized.

You can see from the numbers on Table 6-13 that it really takes 4 wins in a row for you to really start getting ahead:

198   *Winning Systems*

at the end of Play Number 4 you are 5 units up. The 3 win streak at plays 8 thru 10 only nets a one unit win.

Had you been playing one of the systems that called for you to increase your wager after a loss, you would have gotten into deep do-do without even the possibility of profiting from the winning streak.

So far we have only looked at the upside of The Press Then Drag System. There is always a downside. For every potential gain with any system there is always an offsetting penalty, somewhere. Take a look at what happens to a ping-pong session, as shown on Table 6-14.

Table 6-14						
The Press Then Drag System (aggressive)						
Assume a series alternating wins and losses						
Play Number	Amount from Bankroll	Total Wager	Outcome of Wager	Amount on Table	Amount to Bankroll	Net Win
1	-1	1	+	2	0	-1
2	0	2	-	0	0	-1
3	-1	1	+	2	0	-2
4	0	2	-	0	0	-2
5	-1	1	+	2	0	-3
6	0	2	-	0	0	-3
7	-1	1	+	2	0	-4
8	0	2	-	0	0	-4
9	-1	1	+	2	0	-5
10	0	2	-	0	0	-5
11	-1	1	+	2	0	-6
12	0	2	-	0	0	-6
13	-1	1	+	2	0	-7
14	0	2	-	0	0	-7

Table 6-14 shows the Press Then Drag System in just about its worst light. An even series of 7 wins and 7 losses, nets a total loss of 7 units.

The problem is, again, that you get further behind by one unit for each isolated win. A win followed by a loss, looks like a single loss to your bankroll. A series containing a string of alternating single wins and losses will eat your bacon while flat-betting the same sequence would result in a push.

In reality, this is a break-even sequence that is turned into a loss by trying to multiply consecutive wins. If you have no consecutive wins you have nothing to multiply. Worse yet, you have to pay the piper for the attempt.

This Press Then Drag System together with its close cousin, which is coming up next, are probably the most widely played systems in the entire universe of gambling. They are not without merit; nor are they without cost. They merely increase the action, by pushing the betting to a higher level. With an adequate bankroll, they can be put into practice without getting the player into a great deal of trouble, provided the player isn't swimming upstream against a significant House Percentage, or, better yet, played when the player has the edge.

The Drag Then Press System

Systems like The Drag Then Press System try to keep you in the hunt longer by having you recover your initial investment of one unit before you begin increasing your bet along with always having you cut your wager back to one unit after a loss.

The idea is to still allow you to multiply the effect of a winning streak without having you fling yourself onto your sword if the session gets choppy. After the second win in a row, you alternately double up then capture your winnings, as shown on Table 6-15.

Table 6-15						
Drag Then Press System (conservative) Assume 14 consecutive wins and walk away						
Play Number	Amount from Bankroll	Total Wager	Outcome of Wager	Amount on Table	Amount to Bankroll	Net Win
1	-1	1	+	2	0	-1
2	0	2	+	4	2	1
3	0	2	+	4	2	3
4	0	2	+	4	0	3
5	0	4	+	8	4	7
6	0	4	+	8	0	7
7	0	8	+	16	8	15
8	0	8	+	16	0	15
9	0	16	+	32	16	31
10	0	16	+	32	0	31
11	0	32	+	64	32	63
12	0	32	+	64	0	63
13	0	64	+	128	64	127
14	0	64	+	128	128	255

Notice that you need to hit three wins in a row with this system before you begin to forge ahead. After the 4th consecutive win, you are actually only ahead by one unit for each win, but you have 4 units at risk on the table that might turn a profit. After the 6th win in a row, you are in the same situation as after the 4th win, but now you have 8 units on the table working for you. It is only after 7 consecutive wins that you really break into the clear and have profited as by as much as you currently have at risk.

As you can see, the Drag Then Press System is more con-servative than the Press Then Drag Variation: you don't multiply your profits as quickly, but your losses don't add up as quickly either. The alternating sequence of 7 wins and 7 losses, which costs the Press Then Drag version a loss of 7 units, would be a push with the Drag first system.

Take a look on Table 6-16 at the Drag Then Press System under the stress of the now familiar sequence: 1 win, 2 losses, 2 wins, 5 losses, 1 win, 1 loss, then 2 wins.

Table 6-16						
Drag Then Press System (conservative)						
Assume 1 win, 2 losses, 2 wins, 5 losses, 1 win, 1 loss, then 2 wins						
Play Number	Amount from Bankroll	Total Wager	Outcome of Wager	Amount on Table	Amount to Bankroll	Net Win
1	-1	1	+	2	1	0
2	0	1	-	0	0	0
3	-1	1	-	0	0	-1
4	-1	1	+	2	1	-1
5	0	1	+	2	0	-1
6	0	2	-	0	0	-1
7	-1	1	-	0	0	-2
8	-1	1	-	0	0	-3
9	-1	1	-	0	0	-4
10	-1	1	-	0	0	-5
11	-1	1	+	2	1	-5
12	0	1	-	0	0	-5
13	-1	1	+	2	1	-5
14	0	1	+	2	2	-3

Even with this sequence of 6 wins and 8 losses containing a significant drubbing of 5 losses in a row, this Drag Then Press System doesn't do too badly. You just have to have a streak of wins in order for you to come out ahead. In the meantime, the trick is to not get beaten up too badly by being over-optimistic in the face of impending doom.

Both of these last two systems can be played and enjoyed, under the right circumstances. The right circumstances consist of: first, playing the right game, one in which the House Percentage is negligible or where you have the Percentage on your side; second, having a large enough bankroll to ride out the ups and downs, at least a couple of thousand units; and third, understanding that these betting systems do not change the House Percentage or affect your odds at all.

Under these circumstances, adjusting the bankroll requirements appropriately, any of the betting systems we've covered so far, even the ones I consider to be in the Dumb And Dangerous Category are theoretically playable.

The problem with the Dumb And Dangerous Category systems, relative to these, is that the bankroll requirements are enormous: exceeding the amount of money in the known universe.

The Fibonacci Series System (Up Only Variation)

Again, we come to another manifestation of the Fibonacci Series. This variation falls into the category of increasing your bet when you are winning and cutting back when you are losing. After the second win in a row, you get into the progression by betting two units.

Each bet in the sequence is equal to the sum of the preceding two bets. You continue it until the string of wins is broken by a loss and then you cut your wager to one unit.

For a flock of wins, this system shown on Table 6-17 looks just like the other variations.

	Table 6-17					
	The Fibonacci Series System (Up OnlyVariation)					
	Assume 10 consecutive wins and quit					
Play Number	Amount from Bankroll	Total Wager	Outcome of Wager	Amount on Table	Amount to Bankroll	Net Win
1	-1	1	+	2	1	0
2	0	1	+	2	0	0
3	0	2	+	4	1	1
4	0	3	+	6	1	2
5	0	5	+	10	2	4
6	0	8	+	16	3	7
7	0	13	+	26	5	12
8	0	21	+	42	8	20
9	0	34	+	68	13	33
10	0	55	+	110	21	54
11	0	89	+	178	34	88
12	0	144	+	288	55	143
13	0	233	+	466	89	232
14	0	377	+	754	754	986

Showing all these wins in a row is just for the purpose of displaying the system. It is the way, in your dreams, you want it to be in the casino. It's probably never going to happen. Again, the odds are 1 in 16,348. But, it shows you what you are shooting for.

Anytime you plan on running a Fibonacci Series Progression, you should stack up your chips in front of you to show the series: 1, 1, 2, 3, 5, 8, 13, 21... If nothing else, it will confuse the guys who monitor the "eye in the sky" and make the mathematically inclined think that you are one of them. Besides being amusing, it can serve the purpose at the Blackjack table of masking the fact that you are count-ing cards, as described in chapter 3.

Since when you have a loss with the Up Only Variation you cut back to a bet of 1 unit and start over, in the pres-ence of a flock of losses, it looks quite different from the other Fibonacci Series System variations.

Look at what happens with only a few wins in a row, inter-spersed with losses, as shown on Table 6-18 with the old standby sequence: 1 win, 2 losses, 2 wins, 5 losses, 1 win, 1 loss, then 2 wins.

Table 6-18						
The Fibonacci Series System (Up Only Variation)						
Assume 1 win, 2 losses, 2 wins, 5 losses, 1 win, 1 loss, then 2 wins						
Play Number	Amount from Bankroll	Total Wager	Outcome of Wager	Amount on Table	Amount to Bankroll	Net Win
1	-1	1	+	2	1	0
2	0	1	-	0	0	0
3	-1	1	-	0	0	-1
4	-1	1	+	2	1	-1
5	0	1	+	2	0	-1
6	0	2	-	0	0	-1
7	-1	1	-	0	0	-2
8	-1	1	-	0	0	-3
9	-1	1	-	0	0	-4
10	-1	1	-	0	0	-5
11	-1	1	+	2	1	-5
12	0	1	-	0	0	-5
13	-1	1	+	2	1	-5
14	0	1	+	2	2	-3

The results for this sequence with the Fibonacci Series System (Up Only Variation) are identical to that shown in Table 6-13 for the Drag Then Press System: you wind up losing 3 units. Of course, it would have been worse if you hadn't quit with a double win. The deepest trouble you get into here is 5 units down. That's not too bad for a sequence that contains five losses in a row.

This variation of a Fibonacci Series System isn't very dangerous, and like the Drag Then Press System it can be amusing to fool around with when you are not bucking a significant House Percentage, are playing for piddling small stakes and waiting for a chance to pounce. Neither of these systems will guarantee that you will win, in the short-term or the long-term. I can't repeat too often: no system of betting will affect the House Percentage. Even with the Percentage in your favor, there is always an element of risk.

A good example of the trade-off between potential risk and potential reward can be seen if you compare the Fibonacci Series System (Up and Down Variation) with the Fibonacci Series System (Up Only Variation). Applying these systems to exactly the same sets of wins and losses does a pretty good job of illustrating their virtues and flaws.

The idea behind the Up and Down Variation is to take advantage of streaks in both directions and run the risk of taking a big hit if a really monster losing streak occurs. The Up and Down Variation is shown compared to the Up Only Variation on Figure 6-1.

The darker line on Figure 6-1 shows that the Up and Down Variation can perform well during a really dismal session. The lighter line showing the Up Only variation only went down due to the absence of any significant winning streaks, except for the little blip just after 8,000 plays. Bear in mind that both variations are being applied to the same series of wins and losses, just as though two players were betting the same game, just with different betting systems.

Figure 6-1

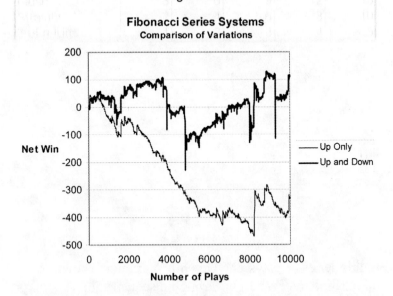

Fibonacci Series Systems
Comparison of Variations

For this session, the Up and Down Variation came out ahead by 115 units after 10,000 plays and was never down by more than 228. The Up Only Variation took a beating of 325 units and was down by 469 units in its depths.

This kind of session is exactly what the Up and Down Variation was intended for. It is a rather miserable streaky session that contains more losses than wins, with only medium length strings of losses mostly broken up by isolated wins. Always bear in mind that the systems that chase a loss will sooner or later come to a bad end, and when they do, it is generally very bad.

Figure 6-2 shows what happens when the "bet more when you are losing" philosophy is struck by its nemesis, a long losing streak.

Figure 6-2

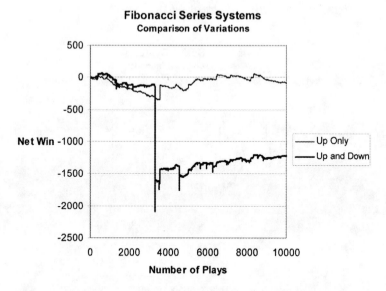

In this series of plays, the Up Only Variation, shown by the lighter line, breezes right through a sequence of 16 straight losses with a drop of only 15 units while the Up and Down Variation, shown by the darker line, went from –113 units to –2,098 units, a 1,985 unit drop. If there had only been 13 losses in a row, the Up and Down Variation would have come out smelling like a rose, but the house limit of 500 units broke its back.

Notice that before the losing streak struck, the Up and Down Variation was again outperforming the Up Only Variation. Up to about 3,300 plays, the rather unremarkable losing session was favoring the Up and Down Variation.

For any system you play, there is always a downside. You should be prepared for Murphy's Law to kick in at any time. If you are, most of these conservative systems can actually be played and enjoyed.

Maturation Systems – It's Overdue

I think that everyone, even the great mathematicians, somewhere deep down have a gut feeling that when something that is reasonably probable hasn't happened in a while, it is overdue. When anything that happens with some frequency hasn't happened in a while, we begin to expect it. As a semi-intelligent species, we evolved by noting and taking advantage of the patterns in our environment: Summer follows Spring; then Fall and Winter, etc. Our universe is full of recurring themes.

If you walk up to a Roulette table, and notice that the tote board shows that a red number has come up the last 15 times in a row, it is only reasonable that you think to yourself: "It's about time for a black to hit. It's overdue." It's the same story at the craps table. If it has been a long time, a lot of rolls, since a particular number has come up, you begin to expect it.

There are about 34 zillion gambling systems based on this human expectation. They are all crap.

Mathematicians will probably always turn purple trying to explain to the uninitiated that random is random, without much success. No matter how much they shout and wave their arms most folks will promptly ignore them, keep stuffing quarters into a ravenous slot machine and say something like: "Well, it hasn't hit in quite a while. I think it's overdue."

It's no matter that the little white ball on the Roulette table has no memory. It doesn't know where it fell last and has no eyes to see the tote board. It is no matter that those little cubes on the craps table don't remember which way was up the last time. Since time immemorial and for all time to come, people have kept, and will continue to keep, studious records of random events to enable them to predict the totally unpredictable.

Hang it up. It ain't gonna happen.

Anytime anyone begins promoting a System or Method of gambling that relies on the outcome history for a game of independent trials, you should avoid them like the plague. Even if they mean you no harm and in good faith really think they are giving you the straight poop, get away from them as fast as you can. Their System or Method will ultimately lead to ruin. It is based on a false premise. Flee!

Note, if you will, that not all games are based on a series of completely independent trials. Some games, card games like Blackjack in particular, under some circumstances are subject to some predictability. The outcome of some card games can be strongly influenced by which cards have been removed from the deck in previous plays. For example, if no aces have been dealt from a regulation deck and the pack is down to four cards, it's probably a good bet that at least one of the last four cards is an ace.

Constrained systems not withstanding, for any random process, any set of independent trials always yields random results. Take it to the bank. The casinos do.

Inertia Systems – When They're Hot They're Hot

The antithesis of the Overdue Systems is the "When They're Hot They're Hot" Systems and the corresponding "When They're Cold They're Cold Systems". Everyone recognizes the concept of "Streaks", hot and cold.

Often, you will hear someone warn a friend: "Don't play that machine, it's cold." The idea that when they are hot, they're hot, and when they're not, they're not has almost as large a following as the overdue baloney. They are both baloney; just slices from opposite ends of the same sausage. Between the two, I tend to lean toward this end. Even the great card mechanic and casino expert, John Scarne, got stuck on this one.

The trap is an easy one to fall into. Even those of us who know better and have had it proven to us time and time again still tend to say dumb things like: "Bet more when you are winning and less when you are losing." when what we really mean to be saying is: "Bet more when you are playing on house money and less when you are playing on your own." It doesn't change the odds; it just tends to keep you from getting emotionally boogered up so badly.

Apparently, it has something to do with inertia. No one expects an avalanche to stop halfway down the mountain. The generation of random sequences of wins and losses, the famous Random Walk, has no inertia.

Only in hindsight is there such a thing as a streak. A clump of wins or losses started when it started and ended when it ended. You can no more get in on the middle of a streak in the here and now than you can go back to yesterday afternoon and get in on one that started then.

I find the Craps tables really amusing, particularly with regard to this bit of superstition. You can always tell when a streak has struck at the Craps tables. On hearing a bunch of whooping and hollering at a Craps table people come running from all over the casino to try to get in on the streak,

like a flock of chickens jumping on a June bug. In the af-
termath, after the sighs of disappointment when the streak
has ended, you will invariably find that the only ones who
profited from the streak were the ones who just happened to
be there when it started.

We human beings apparently haven't evolved to have a feel
for randomness. For most of us, the concept of real randomness appears to be beyond the range of our everyday
comprehension. Those most perceptive amongst us are
closely attuned to cause and effect and have an almost un-
canny knack of knowing what is going to happen next.
That cuts no ice with random systems. By definition, random means you cannot predict what is going to happen
next, no matter how perceptive or smart you might be.

Sorry about that, folks. But there is no such thing as a system that springs from inertia. It is a figment of an overac-
tive imagination: wishful thinking; absolute hogwash. But,
you know that slot machine, over there, by the change
booth has really been paying out ...

Some years ago when I used to play Blackjack early in the
morning at one particular casino, I always sat at a table that
adjoined an alcove where there were a number of unusual
older model video poker machines. Every morning,
promptly at 8:15, a well-dressed older gentleman would
come by and check out the nearly hidden, knee-level, little
pigeonholes where the rejected coins were returned. Going
from machine to machine, he routinely collected a couple
of handfuls of the coins that the players had thought were
lost. As he would depart, with a smile on his face and a
bulge in his pocket, I couldn't help but thinking to myself:
"Now, there goes a man with a Winning System."

Chapter 7 - Money Management

First, you have to have some money to manage. Right there is where the vast majority of all gamblers screw up. Walking up to a $5 table with only a $100 bankroll is like going bear hunting with a billy club. You will need extraordinary luck just to stay alive.

With a really ugly House Percentage staring you in the teeth, the best way to manage your money is to keep it in your pocket. If you play at all, the House is very likely going to get your money. The more you try to stretch out your play, against a big House Percentage, the more likely it becomes.

If you insist on playing against really lousy odds, remember that the casino has a lot more money at their disposal than you do, and you aren't going to get many shots with a small amount of ammunition anyway; so you may as well go out with a bang: bet big. The idea is to hit and run.

Take your time, people-watch or something; and then, just before you are ready to leave the casino, take a deep breath and bet your whole wad in the fewest number of chunks. It will give you the best chance of winning.

With a $20 stake on the slot machines for example, you will stand a better chance – all other things being equal – if you play on higher denomination machines. Rather than playing 400 nickels or 80 quarters, try 20 one-dollar coins. Better yet, use four $5 tokens. To get the best odds of winning, go to the high roller area and bet it all at once with a $20 slug and, if you get anything back, quit. Staying quit is the hard part. For the hit and run strategy to work against lousy odds, you really do have to run when you get ahead.

Bankroll Requirements

For those who aren't intent on being plucked, finding the action with the best Percentage is the critical factor in determining how to best manage your bankroll. Unlike when the Percentage is heavily against you, if you are playing a game in which neither side has an edge, or if you have the edge, the appropriate bet size can be determined precisely.

Over-betting or trying to win a lot with a little is invariably suicidal. Being under bankrolled is a major aspect of Gambler's Ruin. Even with a favorable Percentage, there is going to be considerable back and forth. Over-betting or not having enough of a bankroll to withstand the inevitable bad streak, which will occur from time to time, is certain to put you out of the gambling business.

For an even game, the numbers on Table 7-1 make the point very clearly: The bigger your bankroll is, the smaller is your risk of getting beaten. (Again, the rich get richer.)

Table 7-1				
Gambler's Ruin				
Assume various bankrolls to win 20 units in an even game				
Player's Bankroll	Win Target	House Percentage	Probability of Ruin	Average Number of Plays
5	20	0%	80.0%	100
10	20	0%	66.7%	200
20	20	0%	50.0%	400
30	20	0%	40.0%	600
40	20	0%	33.3%	800
50	20	0%	28.6%	1000
100	20	0%	16.7%	2000
200	20	0%	9.1%	4000
300	20	0%	6.3%	6000
500	20	0%	3.8%	10000
1000	20	0%	1.961%	20000

My computer and my personal experience tell me that, with an even game, if you do it right, about one-third of the time you will come out ahead, one-third of the time you will lose and one-third of the time you will break even. Counting it down to the last chip, about half the time you win; half the time you lose; provided you don't do something dumb.

There are a number of rules-of-thumb which say something like: "Divide your total bankroll into 5 session stakes and keep your bets small enough so that 20 losses in a row wouldn't break you during a single session." In reality, they all say the same thing: for an even game you need a big bankroll relative to your average bet size.

There is much argument and confusion even amongst successful professional gamblers and mathematicians over just what constitutes a big enough bankroll and how to manage it properly to minimize the risk of going broke. Part of the problem has to do with exactly how much risk you are willing to accept. What constitutes a "reasonable" probability of not going broke?

Remember, even with the odds heavily in your favor, there is always some chance of going broke. If you insist on there being no chance of going broke, then you should have an infinite bankroll. Murphy is alive and well, thank you.

Folks who base their minimum bankroll estimates on the probabilities of doubling the stake are, for the most part, talking about a session bankroll, whether they realize it or not. Guidelines which allow for a significant probability of going broke are a recipe for disaster. If your life depended on never going completely broke, how many session bankrolls that stood a 25%, a 10% or even a 5% chance of ruin would you need to have to feel safe?

Judges and juries tend to get all tangled up in their shorts when they get down to defining what constitutes a "reasonable doubt". Mathematicians tend to talk blithely about the meaning of various confidence levels. Usually they will say something like: "Well, the 95% confidence level is pretty much beyond a reasonable doubt." But when you get down to it, it all depends on whose life you are talking about, yours or theirs. The defense team and the prosecution can seldom agree.

The mathematicians have a point, though. There is always an element of risk. If you are going to play, you have to accept that. Hopefully, if you lose your session bankroll, you can always come up with another.

To give yourself the best chance of winning over the long term, the Percentage determines the answer to the question of what size bets you should make relative to the size of your bankroll. For each of the three possible cases, the mathematics are very clear on this point.

If the Percentage favors the house, the absolutely correct answer is: zero. If neither side has an advantage, you need to have a whole lot more money than the other guy. If you have the Percentage in your favor, the correct answer is: never bet more than your % Edge times your total bankroll.

Optimum Bet Size

When the Percentage is in your favor, you should bet as little as possible, relative to your bankroll. It gives the mathematics the best chance to make you a winner. However, you don't want it to take forever for you to win a significant amount. For a game that pays off one to one, mathematicians have worked out that the Optimum Bet

Size, when the Percentage is in your favor, is about the % Player's Edge times the player's bankroll. For example if you have a bankroll of 100 units and an advantage of 1%, you should bet 1 unit.

It's actually a bit trickier than it sounds.

First, it assumes that you have the edge in a game that pays one to one, not variable amounts depending on the intricacies of the game. With Blackjack for example; adding in the effects of doubling down, splitting and getting the occasional Blackjack; the risk and the pay out are not exactly one to one so the Optimum Bet Size gets scaled down by about one-fourth. That makes the optimum bet about 0.75 times the Percentage times your bankroll. If you figure your advantage is 0.5% and your bankroll is $1,000, then your optimum bet would be about $3.75.

Second, your bankroll changes with every win or loss so your Optimum Bet Size changes for every play. With the Blackjack example, if your bankroll shrank down to $100 your Optimum Bet Size would be about 37.5¢. As your bankroll gets smaller and smaller, the optimum bet size never quite reaches zero, which assumes you should be able to make infinitely small fractional bets to avoid going broke. The casinos tend to frown on that.

The Optimum Bet Size, with its conditions properly applied, gives the maximum amount you should bet to get the quickest return that is safely possible. However since the conditions don't really reflect anything approaching reality on this planet, the results of the calculation should be viewed with considerable caution. Cutting this number in half is safer and surer. Even mathematicians generally recommend that you err on the side of caution.

If you think the bankroll size this infers is altogether too large, don't argue with me. Argue with all those dumb mathematicians. Bear in mind that the "take" or "drop" on the Blackjack tables is between 10% and 15% of all money wagered and the theoretical House Percentage is as low as 0.15%, even without counting cards.

Quit While You Are Ahead

No discussion of money management is complete without that old standby: "Quit while you are ahead." It is good advice, provided you can get ahead. It is a standard joke, whenever someone joins a game and wins a small wager on the first play, for some wit to tell them that they should quit while they are ahead.

It is hard to argue with the logic that if you always quit as a winner, you can't lose. It is getting there that is sometimes difficult. Sometimes it seems that you just drop off into a bottomless pit. If you are going to continue to play; that is, come back some other time and take another shot at it, exactly when you quit, ahead or behind, doesn't affect the odds at all. The only thing it is likely to affect is your psyche. I know I sleep better when I quit when I'm ahead.

As far as I am concerned, good money management, or whatever you call it, simply consists of not doing anything dumb and following two simple rules. First, don't play against lousy odds. It may be the only game in town, but you don't have to play it. Second, when you have the odds in your favor, size your bets according to the Percentage and your bankroll. Always remember that your bankroll size is a critical factor. Money is ammunition. Don't leave home without it.

Chapter 8 – Facts, Fallacies, Misconceptions and Outright Lies

The Facts: For the past several years, the casinos in the U.S. have been doing some serious plucking. The numbers are huge. In 2003, U.S. casinos had gaming revenues, which is to say they won, nearly $28 billion. That's billion, with a "B"; definitely not chicken feed.

Table 8-1

Year	Annual US Casino Revenue (in Billions)			
	US Casinos	NV Casinos	NJ Casinos	Other States
1996	17.1	7.4	3.8	5.9
1997	18.2	7.8	3.9	6.5
1998	19.7	8.1	4.0	7.6
1999	22.2	9.0	4.2	9.0
2000	24.5	9.6	4.3	10.6
2001	25.7	9.5	4.3	11.9
2002	26.5	9.4	4.4	12.7
2003	27.9	9.6	4.5	13.8
*2004	29.0	9.7	4.6	14.7

Sources: American Gaming Association, Christiansen Capital Advisors,

Nevada Gaming Control Board, New Jersey Casino Control Commission

* Estimates

Casinos win about 40% of the entire legal gambling take in the United States. Surprisingly enough, Lotteries account for only about 28% of the total U.S. Gaming Revenue. The balance is from Pari-Mutuels, legal Bookmaking, charitable Bingo, etc., according to Sebastian Sinclair, Vice President, Christiansen Capital Advisors, in his testimony before the Subcommittee on Oversight and Investigations of the House Committee on Financial Services, July 2001.

In spite of the healthy revenues, apparently the casino business is not quite all beer and skittles. Although Trump Hotels, Inc. includes three New Jersey casinos that took in a little over a billion dollars in gaming wins in 2003, nearly one-quarter of New Jersey's gaming revenue for the year, they still couldn't come out ahead. According to Timothy L. O'Brien and Eric Dash, of the New York Times New Service, May 3, 2004: "Trump Hotels has never been profitable since it became a public company in 1995."

The failure to turn a profit has not prevented Donald Trump from collecting a salary of $1.5 million a year. With a salary of a $1.5 million a year and gaming revenues exceeding a billion a year to work with, I'm sure I could do as well with a bag over my head.

Of course casinos have to pay their employees and take care of operating expenses. The American Gaming Association is quick to point out that employee salaries alone account for a little more than 40% of the average US casino's total income, and taxes eat up another 15% right off the top. The "nut", the amount most large, heavily financed casinos have to make just to stay in business, is truly awesome. It is like Everett Dirkson once said about the U.S. Budget: "A billion here, a billion there, after awhile it adds up to real money."

The New Jersey Casino Commission is quite forthcoming about financial data on each of the twelve Atlantic City casinos, how much they each win, payroll, expenditures etc. But they aren't quite so generous with the detailed breakdown of exactly how the sheep are shorn.

The Nevada Gaming Control Board, on the other hand, publishes some fairly detailed information on which games make how much money. Not only do they break the Gaming Revenue (meaning: Money Won) down region by region but also by the size of the casino. However, for financial information on specific casinos you need to check their Annual Reports and various SEC filings.

Some fairly interesting facts fall out of the Nevada GCB reports. Casinos have some pretty good tools to work with. The slots and table games bring home some fine looking bacon, as seen on Table 8-2.

Table 8-2

2003 Nevada Gaming Revenue by Type of Game				
Game Type	No. of Units	Annual Revenue	Win per Unit	% Win
Table Games				
Blackjack	3,331	$1,160,890,000	$348,511	13.07
Craps	436	$414,080,000	$949,725	13.24
Roulette	441	$279,368,000	$633,488	23.71
Three Card Poker	178	$127,757,000	$717,736	25.39
Baccarat	91	$406,206,000	$4,463,802	17.40
Mini Baccarat	135	$177,453,000	$1,314,467	13.45
Keno	185	$69,463,000	$375,476	27.43
Caribbean Stud	75	$40,398,000	$538,640	28.92
Let It Ride	149	$66,201,000	$444,302	21.18
Pai Gow	42	$24,409,000	$581,167	19.41
Pai Gow Poker	300	$124,034,000	$413,447	22.41
Table Games Total		$2,890,259,000		
Slot Machines				
1 Cent	6,842	$223,706,000	$32,696	8.35
5 Cent	50,115	$1,404,094,000	$28,017	7.88
25 Cent	61,146	$1,915,335,000	$31,324	5.53
1 Dollar	26,238	$1,221,344,000	$46,549	4.66
Megabucks	665	$58,073,000	$87,328	8.34
5 Dollar	3,216	$244,908,000	$76,153	4.42
25 Dollar	502	$58,655,000	$116,843	3.56
100 Dollar	294	$54,711,000	$186,092	4.36
Multi Demonination	29,972	$1,144,653,000	$38,191	4.87
Slot Machine Totals		$6,325,479,000		

Source: Nevada Gaming Control Board

Slot machines account for nearly two-thirds of Nevada's gaming revenue, table games for almost 30% and the balance is from activities like Bingo, Sports Books, etc. The column labeled % Win on Table 8-2 is interesting, but it doesn't mean quite what you would think it should.

For table games, the % Win is the "hold" or "drop". It is the percentage of chips sold at the table that are kept at the table. It measures how much of the players' cash-in money they eventually walk away with. The balance is the percentage of chips that are cashed in at the cashier's cage.

The number is very sensitive to the amount of money the players choose to cash in with, regardless of how much they wager and how much of it is just for show. On some games, some players just take out a little at a time and lose that amount before they take out more. From the % Win on Roulette being nearly 24%, it is obvious that the number is not exactly the same as the overall House Percentage, which is a solid 5.3%.

The table game 'hold" or, as the Nevada Gaming Control Board calls it, the "Percent Win" reflects the effect of the House Percentage grinding away at the players' bankrolls; the net effect of Gambler's Ruin. It is not the same thing as the House Percentage.

For the Slot Machines, which include Video Poker for accounting purposes, the % Win is closer to the House Percentage. Here, the Percent Win is the percentage of the coin-in, the total amount wagered, that the casino keeps.

Different Points of View

The amount of your money the casino keeps is, for the casino, what it is all about. The figures show that the casinos are very good at taking the players' money. Whether or not they get to keep very much of it depends not only on how well they run their business but how well they fend off others, like various government entities, who absolutely insist on being cut in on the action.

Not only do the various local, county, state and federal governments usually feel that the casinos are sucking up discretionary money that they could have gotten, but a host of other outfits and individuals try to belly up to the trough on a regular basis. Some are more successful than others. Sometimes you can see them coming from miles away.

As long as the economy can afford it, and the politicians and moral reformers are sufficiently appeased, then the commercial gambling establishments, or the Gaming Industry as they prefer to call themselves, are probably here to stay. When the political smoke and mirrors begin to reflect genuine social concerns, fundamental change is possible, but, for the most part, things like government studies are little more than a few sharp elbows at the trough. It seems everyone is always trying to propagandize everyone else to achieve their own ends.

The casinos are pretty good at holding their own. A study financed by Harrah's Entertainment, Inc., entitled Profile of the American Casino Gambler: Harrah's Survey 2003, for example, is a real hoot. Every year or so Harrah's pays big bucks to the Roper polling outfit and NFO WorldGroup to dig up insightful information about the elusive casino gambler. They have succeeded big time.

Their report points out that American casino gamblers, who comprise about 25% of the adult population, are better at saving and handling money than non-gamblers. Gamblers tend to take more vacations, are more widely traveled, eat out more often, indulge in more forms of recreation, own more computers, are more computer literate, are slicker bargain hunters and are wealthier than non-gamblers. Gamblers are also smarter, prettier and smell better than non-gamblers. Ok, I made up the last three. But, being a gambler, I tend to agree with everything they say.

Other reports tend to represent other interests. When the going gets tough and the elbows get sharp, the interested parties tend to call out the big guns. They, in turn, have their own interests to represent.

The National Research Council in its milestone report, Pathological Gambling - A Critical Review (1999) has observed: "the act of gambling has been considered by various observers to provide evidence of recreational interest, diminished mathematical skills, poor judgment, cognitive distortions, mental illness, and moral turpitude." Well, one out of five isn't bad. Or, as Pat Paulson would say: "Picky, picky, picky... "

That is not to infer that problem gambling is trivial. It isn't, but there is a big difference between recreational interest and things like cognitive distortions, mental illness, and moral turpitude. Even if you don't gamble well, it doesn't necessarily mean that you are seriously defective.

 While losing a wager or two from time to time can be considered to be unfortunate, losing repeatedly begins to look like carelessness, at best. Gambling is one of those subjects, like sex and religion, on which points of view are relative to the positions of the observers. There is hardly such a thing as an unbiased observer.

Even the prestigious National Research Council (U.S.), Committee on the Social and Economic Impact of Pathological Gambling can get it wrong. In trying to objectively wrestle down the subject of pathological gambling, they get into the various definitions of gambling. Then to take the middle road, they say: "As used in this report, the term "gambling" refers both to games of chance that are truly random and involve little or no skill that can improve the odds of winning, and to activities that require the use of skills that can improve the chance of winning."

So far so good, that sounds fairly objective. They continue with: "By its very nature, gambling involves a voluntary, deliberate assumption of risk, often with a negative expectable value."

Can't argue with that either, but then they blow it with: "For example, in casino gambling the odds are against the gambler because the house takes its cut; thus, the more people gamble, the more likely they are to lose."

Their assertion that "in casino gambling the odds are against the gambler" is simply not true, at least not always. If you play Blackjack skillfully enough or play one of the 100% plus Video Poker machines skillfully enough, the odds are in your favor and the more you play the more likely you are to win.

Working from the viewpoint that there is just no possible way anyone can ever come out ahead, almost automatically leads to unpleasant conclusions about all the participants, all of the time. If you allow that some casino games have a Percentage that favors the skillful player, you might come to a different set of conclusions.

To be fair, perhaps the Committee should have recognized the possibility that casino gambling wasn't intrinsically a losing proposition patronized only by pinheads and mental defectives. By the same token, to be fair to the Committee, they were not charged with examining anything resembling the healthy recreational aspects of gambling.

Everyone, it seems, has an axe to grind, even if it is only philosophical. With flexible facts you can support any view you wish. If the facts don't fit, feel free to make up whatever "facts" you like. It's a fairly popular pastime.

In trying to promote the idea that the House Percentage is insignificant, the casinos and their confederates bend the truth more than a bit. They blithely say that the average player, who doesn't play much, is unaffected by the small House Percentages and harp on the theme that anything can happen over the short term. There is an element of truth there, but it is a biased picture.

Casinos cheerfully publicize the occasional big win and try to leave the impression that big wins are a common occurrence. They use the news media and every means of advertising you can imagine to distribute their propaganda. They spread their message in ways you seldom even think about.

By putting on activities like tournaments, designed to demonstrate that in the short-term luck can predominate over skill, the casinos try to induce a devil may care attitude on the part of the casual player. Getting the players to neglect the low probabilities that are inherent in games that have a high House Percentage directly affects the casinos' bottom line. Selling that point of view to the general public has enormous profit potential.

You have to give them credit. The casinos are good at public relations. There is no dark conspiracy involved. It is just in the casinos' best interest to sell the idea that anyone can be a winner, irrespective of the Percentage.

But, the Percentage does matter. The devil is in the details. There is enough profit in the details so that 18 out of the 20 largest hotels in the world have been built in Las Vegas and paid for by those small House Percentages that don't matter much to the average player.

Not just in the United States, but worldwide, more and more casinos are opening up and prospering. Annual gambling profits, for the casinos, just keep going up. Casinos are not charitable institutions. As Foghorn Leghorn says: "You just can't argue with the figures."

That being said, it appears that we are in a Golden Age of Gambling, for the player. Competition among casinos, which are mostly publicly owned corporations, regulated by local, state, and federal agencies, has fostered a host of gambling establishments that are probably the most player friendly in the entire history of gambling.

There are more choices for the players. The House Percentages, overall, are at historical lows. The games are uniformly honest. Casinos provide a safe and attractive environment. Gaming activities support some of the best non-gaming entertainment seen anywhere. You've got to give them credit. Casinos put on a good show even if they do tend to bend the facts a little.

The casinos are owned and operated by real people, who like everyone else, are just trying to take care of business as best they can. For the most part, they try to take care of their customers as best they can, too. It's like Amarillo Slim says: "You can shear a sheep many times, but you can only skin him once."

One time I was playing Blackjack at a casino where the pit boss was quite friendly and seemed to enjoy making small talk. He kept being amazed by the particularly bad choices a Blackjack player on an adjacent table was making and was keeping me updated about them. Finally he said to me: "I suppose I shouldn't be critical of his play. He's paying for my salary and supporting your entertainment." Then he pulled out a pen and a comp slip and asked him: "Where would you like to have lunch, Sir? The café or the buffet?"

Casino managers and their in-house experts know the odds, the Percentages, the mathematics of all of their games to within a gnat's eyelash. They rely on the numbers. Then, they tell the players to ignore the numbers; that they don't matter. That sounds fishy to me, but what do I know?

The lies we tell ourselves are probably far more damaging than the lies told to us by others. We all harbor illusions. Deep down everyone knows that he or she is special. Sooner or later things have to work out for the best. Good things have to happen to good people. All you have to do is trust to luck. Right?

It is amazing to watch people gamble at the casinos and to hear about their theories - no, their absolute bottom line beliefs - about a vast variety of contradictory superstitions. The good luck charms and rituals are countless. On the face of it, the rabbit's feet and miscellaneous mumbo-jumbo are harmless enough, but when they are substituted for skill and judgment, they become potentially dangerous.

Fantasizing is one thing but when you find yourself relying on the improbable, you know you are in deep trouble. Mumbo-jumbo just doesn't cut it. Gambling on any game that you really don't know how to play, gambling when you don't know the Percentage to at least 2 decimal places or just trusting in luck can be a recipe for disaster. As they say: it's bad luck to be superstitious.

If you should find yourself really regretting your casino play, you might need help. You might want to consider Gambler's Anonymous. If your gambling has become destructive rather than fun, maybe you should give it up. Some people just can't gamble without hurting themselves and others they care about.

Don't misunderstand. Everyone hates to lose and everyone loses some of the time. Just because you are regretful about a losing session doesn't mean that you are a problem gambler. If you know that something you did caused the loss, like playing a sucker game, and you can resolve to correct the problem, successfully, then you probably don't have a problem.

Diagnosing and fixing errors in what you play and how you play should be a routine part of your gambling experience. Every time you get beat you should learn from the experience. Every time you win you should understand exactly what happened that allowed you to win, so you can do it again. Session postmortems should be brutally honest. Did you make mistakes, were they big or little mistakes, can they be fixed? How?

You should not chalk up wins to being a superior person or losses to being unworthy. In spite of the beaming self confidence of the winners and the hangdog demeanor of the losers, moral virtue does not enter into whether you win or lose. Winning and losing are simply the consequences of luck and skill. As I mentioned earlier: in gambling, luck is usually the result of arranging to have the Percentage on your side.

Even so, sometimes you win and sometimes you lose. You are not going to improve the situation by lying to yourself. As the sign at the entrance to the library says: "Know the Truth and the Truth shall set you free."

To stand a chance, you have to accept reality, the real facts, not the made-up facts, the rumors or the hunches. If you can't convince the American Mathematical Society, then it probably isn't true.

If the hard work of sorting out the facts from the fallacies, misconceptions and outright lies is too much work for you, the casinos will help you out. All casinos have a stock of pre-addressed, postage-paid envelopes on hand that you may pick up from the cashier's cage. They provide these so that you may mail your money directly in to the casino without having to go to the trouble of gambling.

Or, if you wish, you can just give them your credit card number. With a computer and a modem, you can even pretend that you are actually gambling. It's called an Internet Casino.

Few things have astounded me more than the popularity of Internet Gambling. I just can't figure out why people would do it under the circumstances that currently prevail. Me? Gamble on the Internet? I don't think it is possible for me to get that drunk. Maybe, if I had a lobotomy…

Do you believe that people in the U.S. actually contributed $2.2 billion in the year 2000 and $4 billion in 2002 to the sneaky little low-down weasels who put up web sites called

Internet Casinos? When the numbers are in, Americans are expected to have lost $6.3 billion on Internet gaming in 2003 and perhaps as much as $9 billion in 2004. Can you believe it? Apparently, P. T. Barnum's maxim is alive and well in cyberspace.

But, it is true and Internet gambling is growing like a cancer, at least according to Sebastian Sinclair, in his testimony before congress. In advocating for legalization, regulation and taxation of Internet gaming he says: "By taking this industry from the hands of licensed, regulated suppliers and handing it to criminals a Federal prohibition will likely do more harm than good."

I suppose I'm just jealous of those sneaky little low-down weasels; not that I have criminal tendencies or anything like that. It just never occurred to me that anyone could be dumb enough to give his or her credit card number to someone who is totally anonymous and under no regulatory constraint whatsoever, someone who says: "Trust me, my computer program won't cheat you."

It reminds me of the story of the guy driving his friend home from the golf course who says: "I need to stop for gasoline up here at this corner station." He proceeds to stop and fill up his tank. As he pays the attendant for the gas, he asks: "How about the number game?" The attendant says: "Ok, guess a number between one and ten." The guy thinks for a second and says: "Six." Without batting an eye, the attendant says: "Nope, I was thinking of 2." As they are driving away, the friend asks: "What was that number business about?" The guy shrugs and answers: "If you guess the right number you win some free sex." Amazed, the friend says: "You can't ever win that kind of game." The guy replies: "Well, I've never won, but my wife wins all the time."

Finally, we come to the subject of cheating. Yes, cheating does go on at the casinos. Mostly it is by the players. Occasionally it is by the casino employees. Almost without exception, it is the casino that is the target, not the player. On those rare occasions when a customer is ripped off in a casino, it is most likely by another customer.

Casino employees, dealers to be specific, can occasionally make a mistake and inadvertently cheat a customer. If it should happen to you, complain. The dealer will probably have to call over a pit boss. The pit boss will make it right.

I've seen a dealer deliberately cheat a casino customer only once in my many years of casino play. On that occasion, it was out of frustration on the part of the dealer. He was trying to get rid of an abusive drunk that the pit boss refused to deal with properly. Several other customers also saw the dealer cheating the drunk. None of us complained. We were all glad to see him go.

The dealer was taking a big risk. If the casino had caught him, they would have fired him. It is simply not in their best interest to cheat some yokel out of a few bucks. Besides the probability of losing their gaming license, the casino would probably have to cut the employees in on any scam just to keep them quiet. That could get expensive.

Strange things can happen, but would a casino that can make millions of dollars a month, legally, risk it all on a few ill-gotten dollars? It's not very likely. In spite of the evidence, common sense and the like, there are those who are certain that they have been cheated at the casinos. I rather doubt it. But then, I tend to be skeptical of things like flying saucers and alien abductions too. Cheating, on the part of the casinos, just doesn't make sense.

The Truth

The casinos really don't have to cheat you to beat you. They usually have this little thing on their side that's called: The Percentage.

Whenever you hear someone say something like: "The Percentage really doesn't matter", you should step back, admire the outright opulence of the nearly five hundred or so casinos in the United States and appreciate the power of The Percentage. The casinos never put their trust in luck.

To keep from being plucked like a chicken at the casinos, you need to minimize the House Percentage and, in particular, whenever possible, choose to play only those games that actually give the player the Percentage. If you keep your head together and exercise your sense of humor, you can enjoy yourself without getting hurt. If you play well and wisely, you can always go home will all of your feathers and, once in a while, with some of their money.

Breinigsville, PA USA
28 July 2010
242594BV00001B/177/A